Living Science

www.two-canpublishing.com

Published by Two-Can Publishing,
43-45 Dorset Street, London W1U 7NA

© 2002, 2000 Two-Can Publishing

For information on Two-Can books and multimedia,
call (0)20 7224 2440, fax (0)20 7224 7005, or visit our website at
http://www.two-canpublishing.com

Series concept and design: Wendy Baker and Andrew Haslam
Cover design: Picthall & Gunzi Ltd

'Two-Can' is a trademark of Two-Can Publishing.
Two-Can Publishing is a division of of Zenith Entertainment Ltd,
43-45 Dorset Street, London W1U 7NA

HB ISBN 1-85434-886-8
PB ISBN 1-84301-090-9

HB   3 4 5 6 7 8 9 10 04 03 02
PB 1 2 3 4 5 6 7 8 9 10 04 03 02

MACHINES
Author: David Glover BSc PhD: Mike Hirst; Photography: Jon Barnes; Series Consultant: John Chaldecott;
Science Consultant: Graham Peacock, Lecturer in Science Education at Sheffield Hallam University;
Additional design: Helen McDonagh; Thanks also to: Rachel and Catherine Bee, Elizabeth Bricknell and
everyone at Plough Studios.

ELECTRICITY
Author: Alexandra Parsons; Editors: Mike Hirst and Claire Watts; Illustrators: Diana Leadbetter and Michael Ogden;
Photography: Jon Barnes; Series Consultant: John Chaldecott; Science Consultant: Graham Peacock, Lecturer in
Science Education at Sheffield Hallam University; Additional thanks to: Albert Baker, Catherine Bee, Tony Ellis,
Elaine Gardner, Nick Hawkins, Claudia Sebire and everyone at Plough Studios.

SOUND
Author: Alexandra Parsons; Editor: Mike Hirst; Illustrator: Michael Ogden; Photography: Jon Barnes;
Additional design: Belinda Webster; Thanks also to: Albert Baker, Catherine Bee, Tony Ellis and
everyone at Plough Studios.

Printed in Hong Kong by Paramount

Be Careful! Electricity can be dangerous. All the activities in this book use batteries as the power source.
You should **never** experiment with any electricity, plugs or sockets in your home.

Words marked in **bold** are explained in the glossary.

Contents

Being an Engineer 6
Levers 8
Catapults 10
Linking Levers 12
Pulleys 14
Running Smoothly 16
Belt Drive 18
Gears 20
Gear Drawing 22
Cams 24
Screws 26
Balance 30
Pneumatics 32
Rocket Power 34
Wind and Water 36
Rubber-Band Power 38
Moving Through Air 40
Steam Engines 42
Marble Clock 44
All Kinds of Clock 46
Being a Scientist 50
Static Electricity 52
Simple Circuits 54
Batteries 56
Lighthouse 58
Complex Circuits 60
Light Bulbs 62
Circuit Game 64
Switches 66
Morse Code 68
Circuit Quiz 70

Magnetism 72
Magnetic Power 74
Magnetic Boats 76
Magnetic Earth 78
Magnetic Fields 80
Electromagnetism 82
Making a Motor 84
Working Motor 86
Electric Train 88
Boosting Power 90
Be a Sound Scientist! 94
Sound Waves 96
The Ear 98
Hearing 100
Reflecting Sound 102
Amplifying Sound 104
Travelling Sound 106
Recording Sound 108
Ultrasound 110
Radio Waves 114
Musical Scales 116
Playing Pipes 118
Slides & Air Holes 120
Shake, Rattle & Roll 122
Drums 124
Whirling Rattle 126
Bangs & Hums 128
String Instruments 130
Writing it Down 134
Glossary 136
Index 142

Machines

Humans are the only animals that invent and make machines. We use them to build skyscrapers, lift heavy loads and move faster than the speed of sound. Humans have even made machines that can travel to the Moon.

MAKE it WORK!

You don't have to build robots or space rockets to be an engineer. In fact, engineers often make very simple machines. The projects in this book will show you how some machines are made, what they can do and how they work. They'll also show you some engineering experiments. You might even be able to use the ideas for inventions of your own!

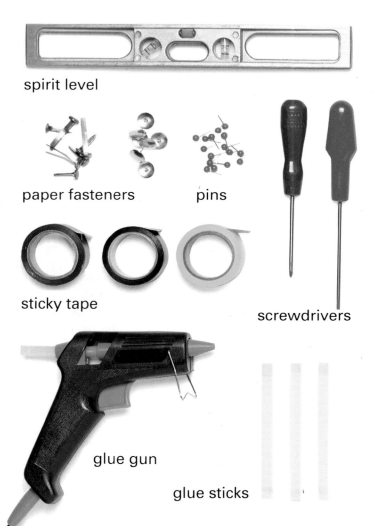

spirit level

paper fasteners

pins

sticky tape

screwdrivers

glue gun

glue sticks

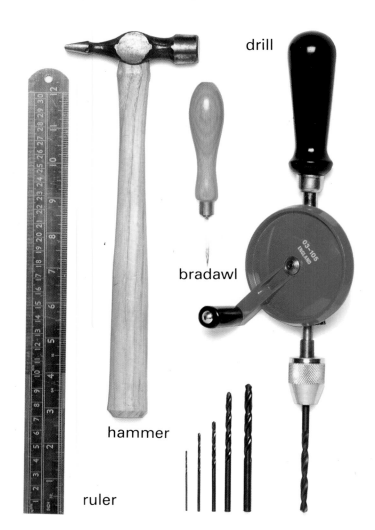

drill

bradawl

hammer

ruler

The scientists who build machines are called **engineers**. They do tests and experiments which help them to invent new machines and make old ones work better. Without engineers we wouldn't have tools or engines, trucks or trains, or even clocks and can openers.

You will need

You can build most of your machines out of simple materials, such as cardboard and balsa wood, plastic bottles and other odds and ends. However, you will need some tools to cut, shape and join the different materials. All of the equipment shown above will come in very handy as part of an engineer's tool kit.

Safety!

Sharp tools are dangerous! Always take care when you use them, and ask an adult to help you. Make sure that anything you are cutting or drilling is held firmly so it can not slip. A small table vice is ideal for holding pieces of wood.

Planning and measuring

Always plan your machines carefully before starting to build. Measure the parts and mark them out with a pencil before you cut. Mark out the positions of holes before drilling them.

Cutting

You will need saws for cutting wood and scissors for cutting card and paper. A sharp craft knife is useful too, but be extra careful with the sharp blade. Use sandpaper or a file to round off any sharp edges.

Drilling

To make some of the machines in this book, you will have to drill holes in pieces of wood. Use a pointed bradawl to start a hole and then finish it off neatly with a hand drill.

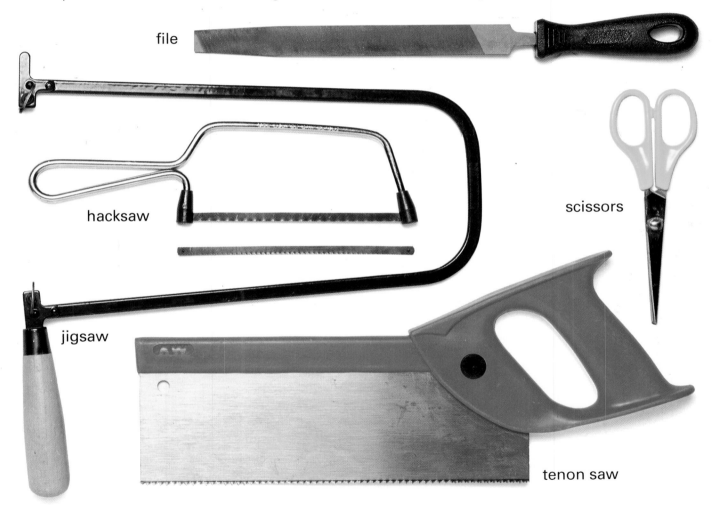

file

hacksaw

scissors

jigsaw

tenon saw

Joining

Strong glue is one of the simplest ways of joining pieces of wood, card or plastic. It's easiest to use glue sticks with a glue gun. Pins, paper fasteners, a hammer and nails, staples and sticky tape are all useful too. A spirit level will come in handy if you want to check that parts are joined straight or level.

Some machines are so simple that we don't always realize they are machines at all. But in fact, a machine is anything which applies a force to do a useful job. A pencil sharpener, for instance, is a machine that uses a turning force to cut wood. Nutcrackers are a machine that uses a squeezing force to crack nuts.

We often use machines to lift heavy weights or to help us move loads from one place to another. A wheelbarrow, for example, is a simple type of lifting machine. We use it to increase the **force** made by our muscles. If you had to move a pile of earth, you could carry a much heavier load in a wheelbarrow than you could lift in your own arms.

Perhaps the simplest machine of all for increasing force is the **lever**. A wheelbarrow is a kind of lever – and many other types of complicated machine are really just collections of levers that are put together to work in different ways.

effort

MAKE it WORK!

A simple lever is a straight rod which rests on a **pivot** or **fulcrum**. When you push one end of the rod down with an **effort**, the other end goes up, lifting the **load**.

Try making this model see-saw and find out for yourself how levers work.

1 Mark the length of wood with paper strips spaced 3 cm (about 1 in) apart.

2 Glue the dowel to the matchbox to make a pivot.

load

pivot or fulcrum

3 Place the centre of the length of wood on the pivot so that the two ends balance.

Now try some experiments with the weights. Put a weight (the load) three marks from the fulcrum. Where must you place another weight (the effort) to lift the load?

More load for less effort!

If the load is close to the fulcrum, it's easier to lift and you don't need so much effort. You may have noticed this if you've ever played on a see-saw – you can lift someone heavier than yourself if they sit nearer to the middle than you do.

Try putting two weights (the load), two marks away from the fulcrum of your see-saw. Where must you put a single weight to lift the load?

To make a see-saw you will need

a length of wood	glue
a small wooden dowel	a ruler
strips of coloured paper	a pencil
weights (washers or coins)	a matchbox

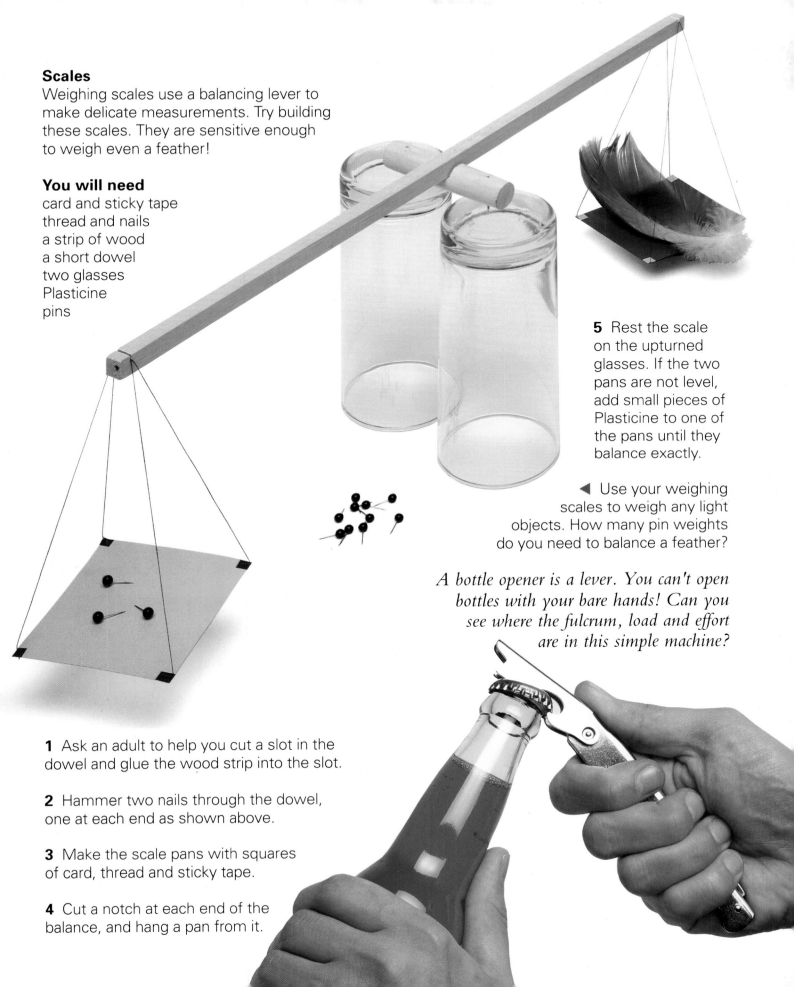

Scales

Weighing scales use a balancing lever to make delicate measurements. Try building these scales. They are sensitive enough to weigh even a feather!

You will need

card and sticky tape
thread and nails
a strip of wood
a short dowel
two glasses
Plasticine
pins

5 Rest the scale on the upturned glasses. If the two pans are not level, add small pieces of Plasticine to one of the pans until they balance exactly.

◀ Use your weighing scales to weigh any light objects. How many pin weights do you need to balance a feather?

A bottle opener is a lever. You can't open bottles with your bare hands! Can you see where the fulcrum, load and effort are in this simple machine?

1 Ask an adult to help you cut a slot in the dowel and glue the wood strip into the slot.

2 Hammer two nails through the dowel, one at each end as shown above.

3 Make the scale pans with squares of card, thread and sticky tape.

4 Cut a notch at each end of the balance, and hang a pan from it.

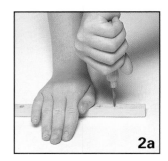 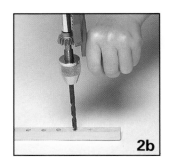

2a **2b**

Have you ever flicked a pea from the end of a spoon? If you have, then you were using a lever. Your thumb was the pivot and your fingers applied the effort, making the bowl of the spoon move quickly, and launching the pea up into the air.

A catapult works in just the same way. Before gunpowder was invented, ancient armies used catapults to fire rocks, burning rags or other **projectiles** at their enemies.

1 Ask an adult to help you cut the baseboard, the two side arms and the main catapult arm from lengths of wood.

2 Drill holes 2.5 cm (1 in) apart along the main catapult arm and the side arms. The holes should be just big enough for the dowel to fit through. Before drilling, mark the position of each hole with a bradawl, as shown above.

MAKE it WORK!
The catapult on this page is powered by a stretched elastic band.

3 Cut the triangular side pieces out of corrugated card. You will need to use a sharp knife, so be careful not to cut yourself.

You will need

a small tin can or plastic pot

thick corrugated card	paint
a thick elastic band	a bradawl
strong wood glue	drawing pins
pieces of sponge	screw hooks
a hand drill	a wooden dowel
wood	a sharp craft knife

4 Glue the cardboard side pieces and the wooden side arms to the baseboard. Then glue the small can or plastic pot to the end of the main catapult arm.

5 Screw three hooks into the baseboard. Use the bradawl to mark the positions of the screws before you twist them in.

*When you fire an object from the catapult, it travels in a curved path called its **trajectory**. The distance the object travels is called its **range**. The range of the object, and how high it goes, depend on its speed and the angle from which it is launched.*

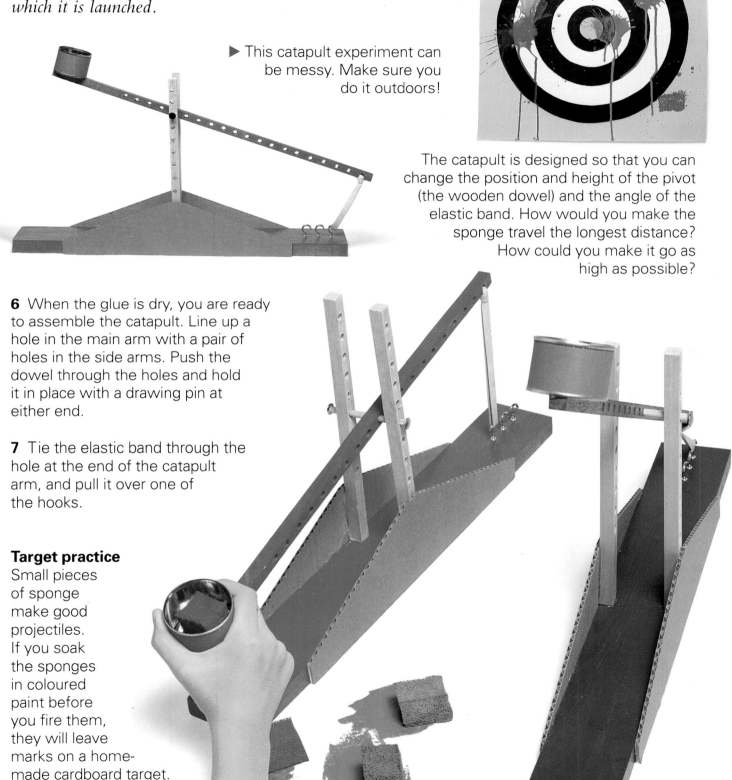

▶ This catapult experiment can be messy. Make sure you do it outdoors!

The catapult is designed so that you can change the position and height of the pivot (the wooden dowel) and the angle of the elastic band. How would you make the sponge travel the longest distance? How could you make it go as high as possible?

6 When the glue is dry, you are ready to assemble the catapult. Line up a hole in the main arm with a pair of holes in the side arms. Push the dowel through the holes and hold it in place with a drawing pin at either end.

7 Tie the elastic band through the hole at the end of the catapult arm, and pull it over one of the hooks.

Target practice
Small pieces of sponge make good projectiles. If you soak the sponges in coloured paint before you fire them, they will leave marks on a home-made cardboard target.

Lifting isn't the only job levers can do. We also use them to change the direction of a movement.

The two ends of a simple lever always move in opposite directions. One end goes up when you push the other end down. By linking two levers with a flexible joint, we can make them move backwards and forwards as well as up and down. Mechanical diggers work in this way – and the bones in our arms and legs are levers, connected at the knee and elbow joints.

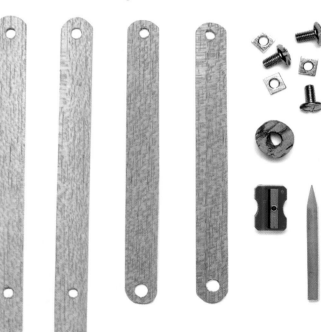

You will need
glue
a cork
sandpaper
a hand drill
nuts and bolts
a pencil sharpener
lengths of balsa wood
a felt-tip pen and paper
a piece of wooden dowel
a drawing board and pins

MAKE it WORK!

A pantograph is a drawing machine made from linked levers. Make one yourself and experiment to see how the linkages work.

1 Cut two balsa-wood lever arms 22 cm (9 in) long and two more 12 cm (5 in) in length. Round the ends of the arms with sandpaper.

2 Drill holes in the levers, just big enough for the bolts to fit through. Begin by making holes at the ends of all four levers.

3 Now drill an extra hole in the middle of each of the two longer levers. If the pantograph is to work well, all the holes must be equally spaced – so be sure to measure carefully and mark the holes with a pencil before drilling.

4 Join the longer levers at one end using a nut and bolt. Then attach a short lever to the middle of each long arm. Don't make the bolts too tight, as all the levers need to move quite freely.

5 Ask an adult to help you drill a hole in the cork, just big enough for the pen to fit through.

6 Glue the cork to the free end of one short lever. Push the pen through it and the free end of the other short arm as shown on the right.

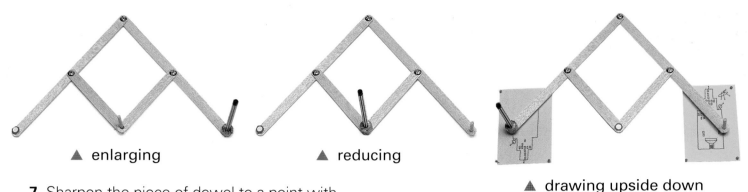

▲ enlarging

▲ reducing

▲ drawing upside down

7 Sharpen the piece of dowel to a point with a pencil sharpener and fix it in place at the end of one of the long lever arms.

8 Place the pantograph on a drawing board and push a pin through the last free hole.

9 Pin the drawing you want to copy under the dowel pointer and fix a blank piece of paper under the felt-tip pen.

10 Trace around the drawing with the pointer and watch how the pantograph's lever arms carry the movement to the pen.

▼ With the pantograph set up like this, the copy is smaller than the original. The short arms are half the length of the long ones, so the copy is just half the size.

*The movements made by linked levers depend on two things: the length of the levers **and** the positions of the joints. A movement can be made bigger or smaller simply by changing the way the lever rods are linked to one another.*

Different drawings
If you swap around the positions of the pin, wooden pointer and felt-tip pen, you can also make the pantograph draw larger, or the same size but upside down. The photographs above show how you should arrange the parts to produce some of these different results with your pantograph.

Pantograph experiments
What do you think would happen if you changed the length of the lever arms? You could experiment by drilling more holes along the arms and then bolting them together in different ways. You may end up with drawings that look stretched, squashed or tilted!

Imagine that you wanted to fix a flag at the top of a tall pole without moving your feet from the ground. How could you do it?

The easiest answer would be to use a **pulley**, fixed at the top of the pole, with a rope looped over it.

A pulley changes a downward pull on one end of a rope into an upward pull at the other end. With simple pulleys we can lift all kinds of loads up poles or tall buildings – and if you have a roller blind at home, you'll be using pulleys yourself every time you pull it up or down.

MAKE it WORK!

Cotton reels make first-class pulley wheels. With a few reels you can make a whole set of pulleys to experiment with.

You will need

some cotton reels
string or cord
yoghurt pots
eye hooks
thick wire
pliers
sand

▲ **Single pulley**

1 Push a piece of wire through the hole in a cotton reel. Use the pliers to cut, bend and twist the wire to make a pulley as shown.

2 Make sure the cotton reel spins freely on the wire and then hang the pulley from an eye hook.

3 Loop the string over the pulley and tie a load to one end. A yoghurt pot filled with sand is a good load. Push a wire through the sides of the pot to make the handle.

Easing the load

Experiment to see how easily you can lift the pot full of sand with your simple pulley. One single pulley won't make it any easier to lift the load, it just changes the direction in which you apply the force. You pull down on the rope to make the load go up. With a single pulley you can not lift anything heavier than you could using just the strength of your arms. However, see what happens if you use two or more pulley wheels together.

◄ Double pulley

1 Make a second simple pulley just like the first, and hook it to the pot handle.

2 Tie one end of the string to the top of the wire hanger on the first pulley as shown.

3 Loop the string under the lower pulley and then back up over the top of the upper pulley.

Now test the double pulley system to feel how difficult it is to lift a load. Do you need to use more force than with a single pulley, or less?

► Quadruple pulley

To make a pulley system with four wheels you will need to make two twin **pulley blocks**.

1 Using a longer piece of wire, make two new hangers, each wide enough to hold two cotton reels, positioned side by side.

2 Tie the string to the top hanger. Loop it down under one of the lower pulleys and then around each of the other pulleys as shown.

How does this system of four pulley reels compare to the simpler ones?

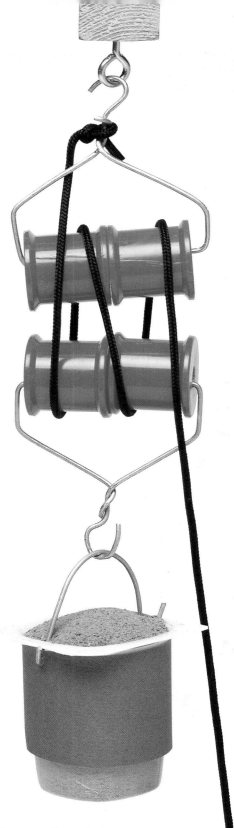

Heavier weights, shorter distances

With two pulleys you can lift almost twice as much as with a single pulley, without using any extra force. But you don't get anything for nothing – the load only travels up half as far as the distance you pull on the string! Four pulleys lift almost four times as much.

Pulley systems work in rather the same way as levers. They help us to lift big loads with just a small effort. With a pulley block, a car mechanic can lift the engine out of a car in order to repair or replace it.

Have you ever been ice skating? Skates glide smoothly across the ice and you move with hardly any effort. Rubber boots, on the other hand, are not slippy at all. They keep a firm grip on the ground, and stop you sliding even if you're walking in slippery mud.

▲ Put some marbles under a tin lid on a smooth surface. The marbles cut down the friction, and the lid rolls around smoothly. Balls that reduce friction in this way are called **ball bearings**.

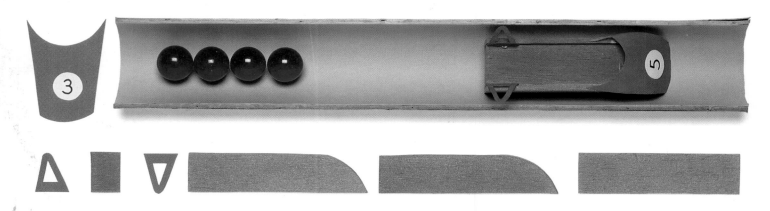

Friction

Rubber boots grip the ground firmly because of **friction**. This is an invisible force, caused when two objects rub against one another. Friction stops things sliding. When rubber rubs against anything, it causes lots of friction. But thin strips of metal on ice make hardly any friction at all.

Bearings

Friction can be a nuisance in machines, and may stop the parts from moving smoothly. Many machines contain ball bearings to cut down on friction. There are ball bearings inside the **hub** of a bicycle wheel. As the wheel rotates, the steel balls turn round inside the hub.

MAKE it WORK!

At the Winter Olympics, bob sleighs hurtle down the icy bob-sleigh run at thrilling speeds. These model bob sleighs don't run on ice – but they can still pick up plenty of speed as they race down their tracks made of card.

You will need

strong wood glue
cardboard tubes
wooden dowels
some marbles
balsa wood
Plasticine
thin card

4 Build a track from sections of tube that are connected with bends of fairly thin card. Hold the track up on pieces of wooden dowel fixed in lumps of Plasticine.

5 Decorate your track with card flags and coloured markers.

6 Place the bob sleigh on the marbles and set it off down the run. The marbles don't make much friction, so the bob picks up speed and will be going fast once it reaches the bottom!

Bob-sleigh races

Build a double run, make two bob sleighs and you can hold competitions. Try adding weights to the sleighs (use lumps of Plasticine) – do the weights make the sleighs go faster?

Ball bearings aren't the only way of cutting down friction. Oil is a good solution too. The slippery liquid spreads out in a very thin layer between the moving parts of a machine. It's a vital part of most engines.

1 Cut out the balsa-wood pieces to make the sides, top and back of the bob sleigh. The bob sleigh should be slightly wider than the marbles, but not quite as deep.

2 Glue the balsa-wood parts together. Cut the nose and the tail fins from thin card and glue them in place.

3 Ask an adult to help you cut some cardboard tubes in half lengthways. (The insides of old kitchen-foil rolls come in handy here, or, if you have some old plastic guttering, you could even use that to make the bob-sleigh track.)

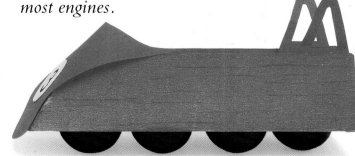

Roundabouts, sewing machines, record players, fishing reels, washing machines and bicycles: these are just a few of the many machines that turn, or **rotate,** as they work.

All the different rotating parts inside a machine can be connected with a **drive belt.** As one part turns, it drags the belt around with it, carrying its turning motion to all the other parts of the machine.

1 Cut the sandpaper into strips, and glue a strip around each of the cotton reels. The rough surface of the sandpaper is needed to make some friction between the reels and the belt. This way, the belt does not slip.

2 Draw both the front and the back of each acrobat on a piece of card as shown, leaving a space between front and back to make a base. Cut out the figures. Then fold and glue them so that they stand up.

3 Glue an acrobat onto each cotton reel.

MAKE it WORK!

A drive belt runs around a series of pulleys, to carry the turning force from one place to another. If the belt is going to work properly, there must be **friction** between it and the pulleys, so that the belt does not slip. If the belt is too slack, it will not grip. If it is too tight, it might break, or twist the pulleys out of line. These whirling acrobats stand on cotton reels, connected by a belt made from ribbon.

You will need

sandpaper
glue and card   a ribbon
a wooden board   cotton reels
sticky-backed Velcro   a wooden dowel

4 Ask an adult to help you cut the wooden dowel into a number of shorter dowel pegs. Smooth the ends of the pegs with sandpaper.

5 Drill holes into the baseboard. They should be just big enough for the dowel pegs to fit snugly into them.

6 Put the pegs into the holes, and then fix a cotton reel onto each peg. Check that every reel can turn around freely on its peg.

7 Push a short piece of dowel into the gap between the centre hole and the rim of one cotton reel. This is the drive belt handle. You will use it to turn the drive belt.

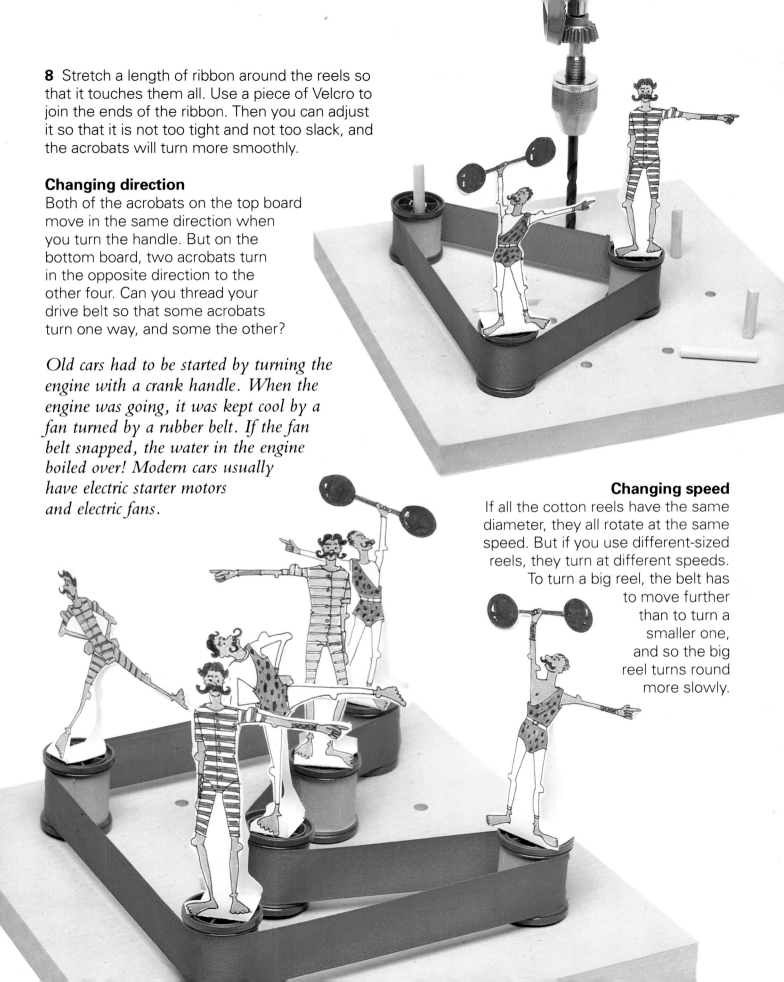

8 Stretch a length of ribbon around the reels so that it touches them all. Use a piece of Velcro to join the ends of the ribbon. Then you can adjust it so that it is not too tight and not too slack, and the acrobats will turn more smoothly.

Changing direction

Both of the acrobats on the top board move in the same direction when you turn the handle. But on the bottom board, two acrobats turn in the opposite direction to the other four. Can you thread your drive belt so that some acrobats turn one way, and some the other?

Old cars had to be started by turning the engine with a crank handle. When the engine was going, it was kept cool by a fan turned by a rubber belt. If the fan belt snapped, the water in the engine boiled over! Modern cars usually have electric starter motors and electric fans.

Changing speed

If all the cotton reels have the same diameter, they all rotate at the same speed. But if you use different-sized reels, they turn at different speeds. To turn a big reel, the belt has to move further than to turn a smaller one, and so the big reel turns round more slowly.

You'll find **gears** inside nearly every machine that turns. Clocks, watches and bicycles all use them. Just like a belt drive, the gears connect all of the rotating parts, but gears last longer than belts and are more accurate. If you've ever ridden a mountain bike, you'll know that gears are a good way of changing speed too.

MAKE it WORK!

The best way to find out how gears work is to make some of your own to experiment with. Each of these home-made gears is made from a jar lid, with a strip of corrugated card stuck around the rim. The corrugations face outwards to make the gear teeth.

1 Bend a strip of card around the rim of a jar lid. Try to stretch it into place so that there is a whole number of teeth evenly spaced around the lid. Cut the strip carefully to length and then glue it in place.

You will need

strips of corrugated card about 1 cm (½ in) wide (You can make these by peeling apart the thick cardboard sides of a cardboard box.)
jar lids and bottle tops of different sizes
a pin board and pins
a short dowel peg
glue and paper

2 Make a small hole in the middle of the gear and pin it to the board so that it spins freely.

3 Make a selection of different-sized gears to add to the board. Glue a dowel peg to one of the gears to make a crank handle.

4 To make the gears work you must place them so the teeth **mesh**. When you turn one gear its teeth will push on its neighbour's teeth and make them turn in the opposite direction.

Gear experiments

Connect a series of gears like the one shown above. If you turn the big gear, what happens to the two smaller ones? Which way do they go around? Which does a complete turn first?

Now try turning the small gear – do the bigger gears turn more quickly or more slowly?

Count the number of teeth on each gear. If you turned a gear with 20 teeth around once, how many times would it turn a gear with 10 teeth?

Drive chains

In some machines, gears called **sprockets** are connected by a **drive chain**. A bicycle chain connects a sprocket on the pedals to another one on the back wheel. The chain transfers the movement from the pedals to the wheels.

▼ Make a model drive chain from a long strip of corrugated card with the ends taped together. Loop it around two different-sized gears and work out how far the small gear moves when you turn the larger one.

Turning gears make beautiful patterns. As a gear goes round, each point on the wheel's surface follows a different path. By tracing these paths, we can draw patterns of loops and curves that repeat and shift as the gear rotates.

1 Use a craft knife to cut a large, circular hole in a square of stiff card.

2 Glue a narrow strip of corrugated card round the inside of the hole. Position the strip so that the corrugations face into the hole to make gear teeth. Make sure that one edge of the strip is level with the edge of the hole, so that the card will lie flat on top of the pin board.

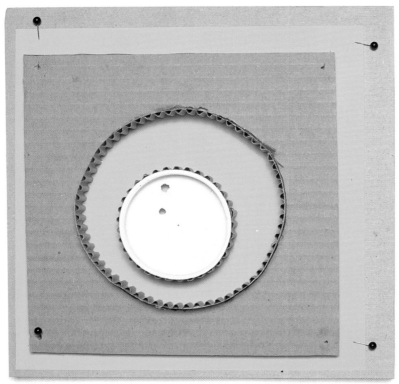

MAKE it WORK!

This gear drawing machine uses the home-made lid and corrugated-card gears from the page before. Experiment with different-sized gears to discover all kinds of patterns.

You will need

pins
a pin board
corrugated card
gears made from lids and card (Gears made from plastic lids are easiest to make holes in.)

drawing paper
a pen or pencil

3 Put a sheet of paper on the pin board and then pin the square with the hole in it on top.

4 Make small holes in your gear wheels at different distances from the centre. The holes must be big enough for the point of your pen to fit through.

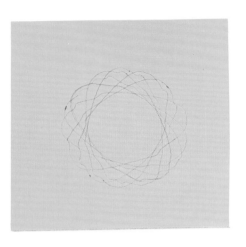 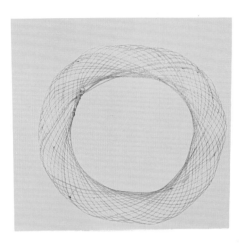 

5 Place a gear wheel in the large cardboard hole and put the point of a pen through one of the small holes so it touches the paper.

6 Hold the board firmly with one hand and use the pen to push the gear carefully around the inside of the large circle. As the gear rotates, the pen draws a line on the paper.

7 Keep pushing the pen and the gear around to build up a beautiful curved pattern.

▲ Try to make some drawings using different-sized gears and with holes that are at different distances from the centre of the gear.

Some patterns will repeat after just a few turns, others may take many turns before they start again. Can you work out if this is anything to do with the number of teeth on the gears or the position of the pen hole? You could also make up a second gear board with a different-sized hole to investigate even more patterns.

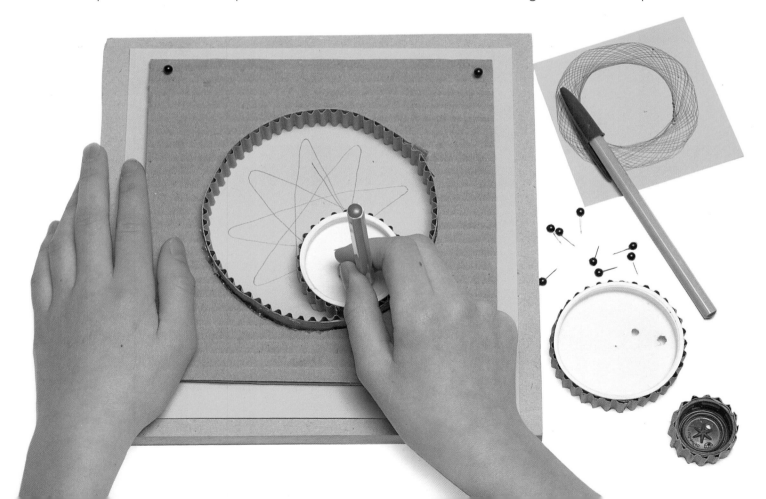

Gears let us transfer movement from one wheel to another, but how do you change a turning movement into an up and down one? The answer is a **cam**.

A cam is like a wheel, but with the **axle** (the shaft that goes through the middle) in the wrong place. If you watch a point on the edge of the cam, it seems to move up and down as the axle of the cam goes round and round.

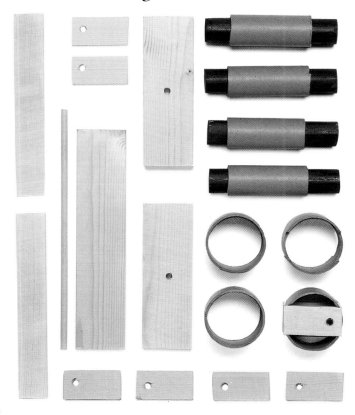

MAKE it WORK!
This model cam shaft shows exactly how rotating cams can move things up and down – and in the order you choose.

You will need
wood	a drawing pin
strong wood glue	thick and thin dowels
two thick cardboard tubes of different widths	

1 Ask an adult to help you cut the pieces of wood needed for the frame which will hold the cam shaft and the four plungers. The height of the frame must be at least twice the diameter of the cams. The plunger tubes must fit tightly into the space across the top of the frame.

2 Cut the wide cardboard tube into four rings. These will be your cams.

3 Cut eight short strips of wood which just fit across the cardboard cams. At the end of each strip, drill a hole with a diameter a little larger than that of the thin dowel rod.

4 Cut slots in the rims of the cams and glue the wooden strips in place as shown. Make sure the holes face each other on opposite sides of each cam.

5 When the glue is dry, push the cams on to the dowel rod to complete the cam shaft.

6 Cut four lengths of the narrow cardboard tube and four, longer lengths of the fatter dowel to fit inside. These will be the plungers.

7 Drill two holes, facing one another, half-way down each of the frame's side pieces.

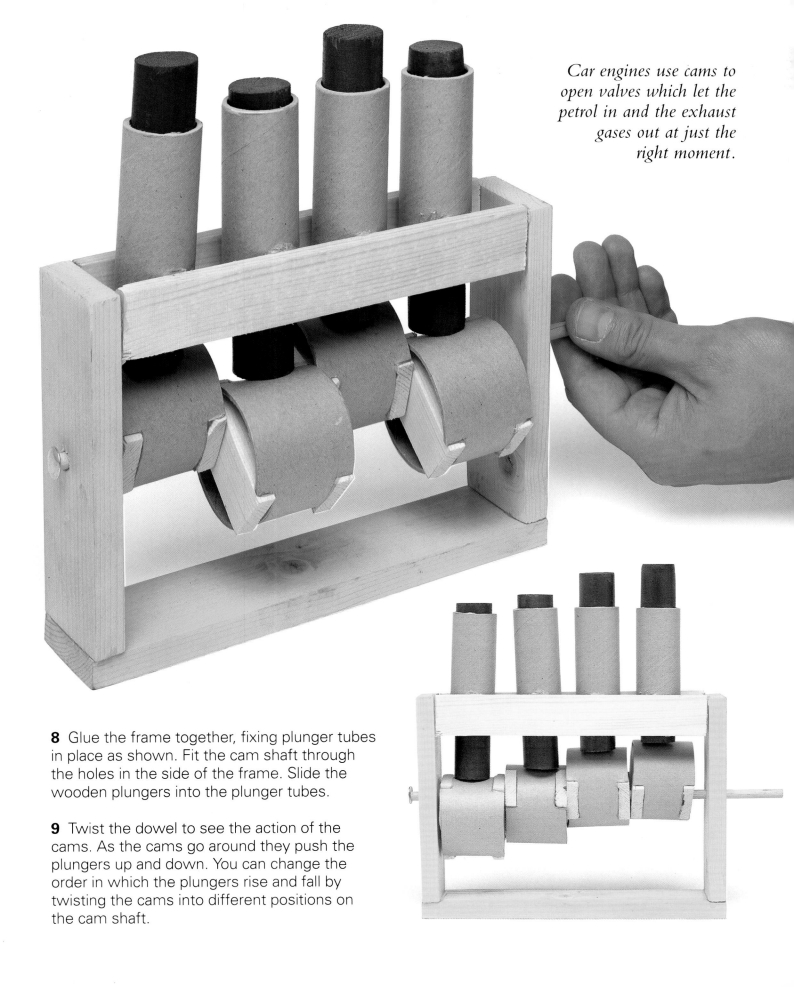

Car engines use cams to open valves which let the petrol in and the exhaust gases out at just the right moment.

8 Glue the frame together, fixing plunger tubes in place as shown. Fit the cam shaft through the holes in the side of the frame. Slide the wooden plungers into the plunger tubes.

9 Twist the dowel to see the action of the cams. As the cams go around they push the plungers up and down. You can change the order in which the plungers rise and fall by twisting the cams into different positions on the cam shaft.

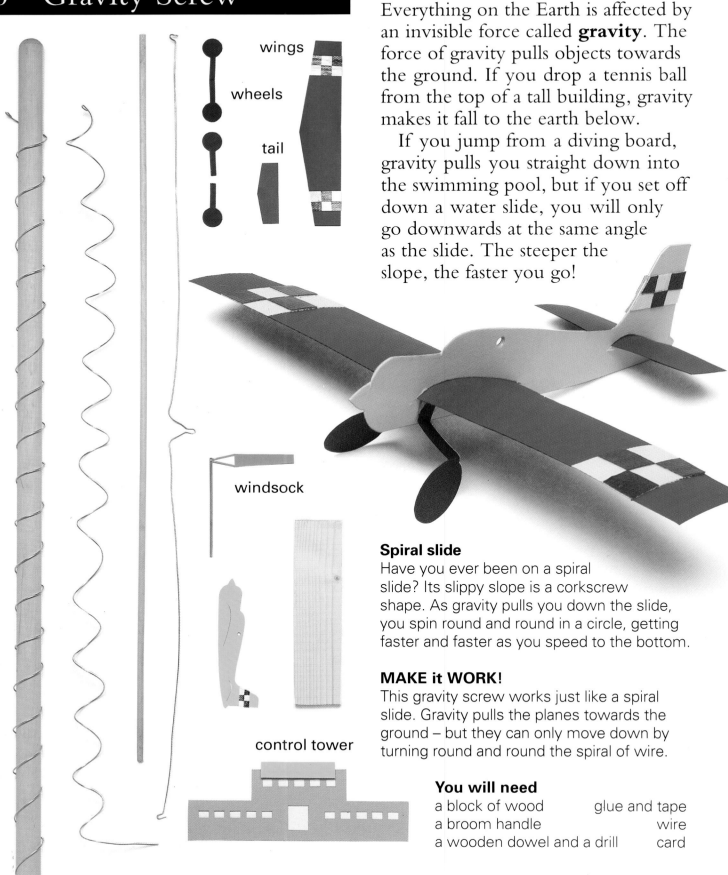

wings

wheels

tail

windsock

control tower

Everything on the Earth is affected by an invisible force called **gravity**. The force of gravity pulls objects towards the ground. If you drop a tennis ball from the top of a tall building, gravity makes it fall to the earth below.

If you jump from a diving board, gravity pulls you straight down into the swimming pool, but if you set off down a water slide, you will only go downwards at the same angle as the slide. The steeper the slope, the faster you go!

Spiral slide
Have you ever been on a spiral slide? Its slippy slope is a corkscrew shape. As gravity pulls you down the slide, you spin round and round in a circle, getting faster and faster as you speed to the bottom.

MAKE it WORK!
This gravity screw works just like a spiral slide. Gravity pulls the planes towards the ground – but they can only move down by turning round and round the spiral of wire.

You will need
a block of wood	glue and tape
a broom handle	wire
a wooden dowel and a drill	card

1 Wind a length of wire around the broom handle to make the spiral. Take care to make the loops of the spiral evenly spaced. Slide the finished spiral off the handle.

8 Hang the planes on the hooks and put the hanger on the top of the spiral. Let it go, and see if it runs smoothly down the spiral. You may need to adjust the shape of the hanger loop and some of the twists in the spiral to get the planes to fly really well.

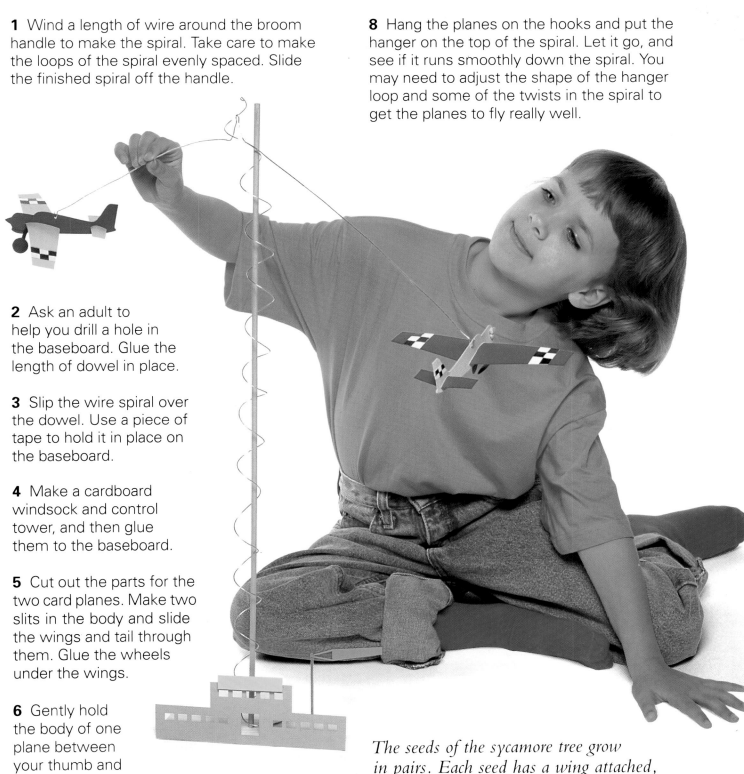

2 Ask an adult to help you drill a hole in the baseboard. Glue the length of dowel in place.

3 Slip the wire spiral over the dowel. Use a piece of tape to hold it in place on the baseboard.

4 Make a cardboard windsock and control tower, and then glue them to the baseboard.

5 Cut out the parts for the two card planes. Make two slits in the body and slide the wings and tail through them. Glue the wheels under the wings.

6 Gently hold the body of one plane between your thumb and finger to find the place where it balances. Make a small hole in the body at this point.

7 Bend a second length of wire into a hanger shape. Make a loop in the middle to fit over the wire spiral and bend small hooks at each end.

The seeds of the sycamore tree grow in pairs. Each seed has a wing attached, which makes every pair spin round as they fall out of the tree. The spinning movement slows down the fall of the seeds, so that they catch the wind and travel further away from the tree before finally settling on the ground.

Spirals and screws come in handy for moving things upwards as well as down. One of the first people to use a screw as a lifting machine was the Ancient Greek scientist, Archimedes. He invented a screw pump that could raise water from a lower level up to a higher one – making it flow against the pull of gravity.

3 Cut a small hole in the centre of each disc, the same diameter as the wooden dowel.

4 Make a slit in each cardboard disc, from the centre hole to the edge.

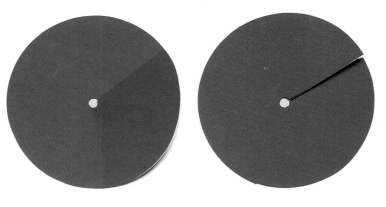

5 Now join the cardboard discs to make the screw shape. Take two discs. Glue the edge of the slit in one disc onto the opposite edge of the slit in the second disc.

6 Next, glue the free edge of the slit in the second disc to the opposite edge of the slit in a third disc.

7 Continue to glue the slit edges in this way until all six discs have been stuck together to make a screw.

8 Push the dowel through the holes in the centres of the discs, and stretch out the screw along the length of the dowel as shown below. Glue the two free ends of the cardboard screw firmly to the dowel.

MAKE it WORK!

This model Archimedean screw is not really strong enough, or made of the right materials, to lift water – but it is an ideal dispenser for popcorn or breakfast cereal.

You will need

a wooden dowel
a sharp craft knife
a plastic soft drink bottle

glue
a drawing pin
fairly stiff card

1 Ask an adult to help you cut the bottom off the bottle and to cut a triangular hole in the neck as shown.

2 Cut out six cardboard discs, just big enough to fit inside the plastic bottle.

9 Slide the completed screw into the bottle. Hold it in place with a drawing pin pushed through the bottle top and into the end of the wooden dowel.

10 Now test your Archimedean screw. Dip the bottle in a bowl of popcorn and twist the dowel gently with your fingers to draw some popcorn up out of the bowl.

Archimedean screws are used in combine harvesters to lift the grain into storage containers.

▲ Just like cams, screws are a way of changing one kind of movement into another. Our popcorn dispenser changes rotation (twisting the dowel) into upward movement.

Although Archimedean screws were first built more than two thousand years ago, they are still used today. In some parts of Africa, farmers use them for irrigating their crops. The screws lift water out of rivers into raised irrigation channels. These ancient water pumps are powered either by animals, such as bullocks, or by hand.

Because gravity pulls things towards the ground, it is much simpler to stay on a trapeze than it is to balance on a high wire. A trapeze artist's weight hangs below her hands, so, as long as she has strong arms and holds on tight, she won't fall off. But a tightrope walker's weight is all above her feet – she only has to lean over a little and she topples from the wire.

MAKE it WORK!

Try making these simple balancing toys. They seem to stand above the wire, but they work because really most of their weight is hanging below it.

To make balancing acrobats you will need

stiff card	coloured pens
small metal washers	glue and scissors

1 Draw an acrobat on a piece of card. The left-hand side should be a mirror image of the right.

2 Cut out the acrobat. Cut a small notch in his hat where he will balance on the wire.

▲ A **pendulum** bob hangs with its weight as low as possible. If you push it aside, the force of gravity pulls it back again.

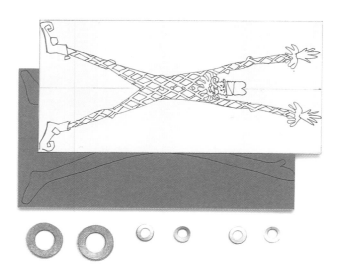

3 Glue a washer to each of the acrobat's hands.

The weight of the washers below the wire helps the acrobats to balance above it.

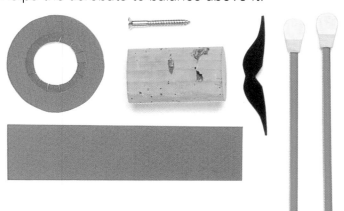

Some tightrope walkers carry a long, flexible pole. It helps to keep their weight low, just like the moustache men's knitting needles.

Gyroscopes

A gyroscope is a machine which seems to defy the force of gravity! It has a heavy metal disc, which spins around on an axle inside a frame. Although gravity still pulls the machine down, the spinning movement of the disc stops it from toppling over, and so the gyroscope balances on the wire.

◀ balancing acrobats   ▶ gyroscope

◀ moustache men

To make moustache men you will need

knitting needles
brass screws
scissors
corks
card
glue

1 Cut out the card moustache and hat pieces. Glue them on the cork as shown.

2 Twist a screw into the bottom of the cork.

3 Ask an adult to help you push two knitting needles into the cork at an angle.

Just like the acrobats, the moustache men balance because most of their weight is in the knitting needles, below the wire.

▶ Setting a simple gyroscope spinning.

A gyroscope has a very useful feature – once it is spinning, the axle will keep on pointing in the same direction so long as it is allowed to move freely. In the early twentieth century, scientists used this feature to develop a new kind of compass – the **gyrocompass**, *which is used in most ships and aircraft today.*

Pneumatic machines use air to transfer force from one place to another. We tend to think that air is weak and thin, but if it is squashed together, or **compressed**, it can push with tremendous strength. A hurricane, for instance, can blow down trees and buildings. The air inside an air-bed will hold up the weight of a person. And a tyre filled with air can carry the weight of a huge lorry or a jumbo jet.

MAKE it WORK!

This pneumatic man is fired by squeezing the plastic bottle to compress the air inside. The air is pushed out along the straw and launches the flyer like a human cannon-ball.

You will need
card and thread
a washing-up liquid bottle
a plastic bag
a thin straw
a fat straw
sticky tape

1 Seal one end of the fat straw with a piece of tape.

2 Cut out the shape of the man in thin card and stick him to the sealed end of the straw.

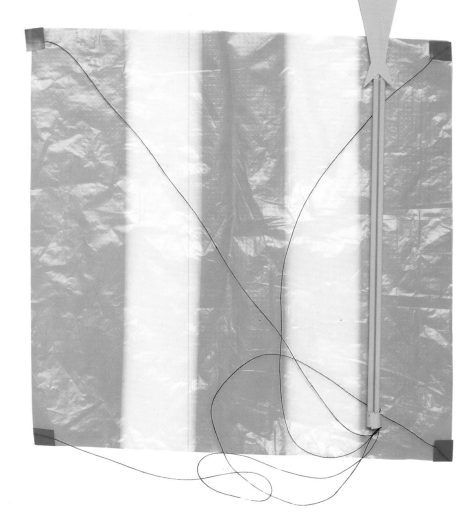

3 Push the thin straw onto the nozzle of the washing-up liquid bottle. If it does not fit very well, seal the join with Plasticine or glue.

4 Slide the fat straw over the thin straw. If the fat straw doesn't fit neatly, cut a slit up its side and pull it a little tighter around the thinner straw. Then seal it up again with sticky tape.

5 To test the pneumatic man, squeeze the bottle sharply. The compressed air inside the bottle pushes against the sealed end of the thick straw as it tries to get out. The flying man is launched along a curved **trajectory**, like the sponges launched from the catapult on page 9.

Parachute

If your man is a high-flyer, you could equip him with a parachute so that he has a soft landing.

1 Cut an 18 cm (7 in) square sheet from a plastic bag.

2 Tape an equal length of thread to each corner of the plastic square. Then tape all the free ends of thread to the base of the fat straw.

3 Fold the parachute into a strip and lay it alongside the straw.

4 Launch the man in the usual way. The parachute will unfold and bring him gently back down to the ground.

▶ As it comes down, the open parachute fills with air. Air pushing upwards underneath the plastic slows down the man's fall, just as it would slow the fall of a paper tissue or feather.

Pneumatic tyres

Pneumatic tyres are tyres filled with compressed air. Before they were invented, carts and bicycles had simple tyres made from solid rubber strips. Pneumatic tyres are a great improvement because they are springier, and so give a much more comfortable ride than solid rubber.

Pneumatic tyres were invented by John Dunlop in 1888. He had the idea for them when he saw his son riding a tricycle over a piece of rough ground. Dunlop made his first air-filled tyre from a length of rubber garden hose. The company he founded still makes tyres today.

All machines need **energy** to make them go. Our pulleys were turned by human muscle energy. The gravity screw worked by the downward pull of gravity on the plane. But most big machines today are driven by **engines**.

An engine makes power by burning a fuel such as petrol or coal. Burning the fuel releases the energy it contains. A rocket engine works by burning the rocket fuel so that it squirts hot gases backwards at great speed. As the gases push back, the rocket is thrust forwards and shoots up into the sky.

MAKE it WORK!

This water rocket isn't powered by rocket fuel, but it does work in a similar way to a real rocket using just air and water. The space above the water is pumped full of compressed air with a bicycle pump. Eventually, the energy stored in the squashed air pushes the water out of the base, and the rocket is thrust up off the ground.

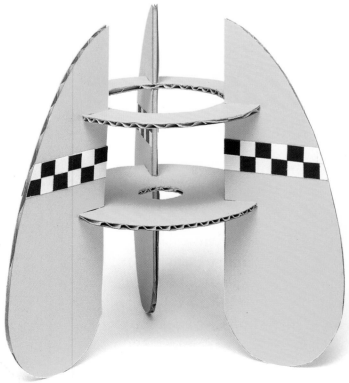

To make a water rocket you will need

strong glue
a bicycle pump
thick, corrugated card
an air valve (The kind that is used for blowing up footballs is best – you can buy one at a good sports shop.)

sticky tape
a rubber bung
a plastic bottle

Be very careful!
This rocket is very powerful and could hurt someone seriously if it hit them. **Never** launch it without an adult to help you.

- **Always** fly the rocket out of doors in a wide empty space, well away from roads.
- **Never** fly the rocket near other people.
- **Don't** stand over the rocket as you pump it up. Keep well to the side.

1 Cut the three base fins, two base rings and three nose-cone parts from corrugated card.

2 Make the rocket base from the fins and the two rings as shown. Stick the parts together with tape or strong glue. Then glue the base onto the plastic bottle.

3 Make the nose cone and fix it in place on top of the rocket.

4 Ask an adult to help you make a small hole through the rubber bung with a pin or a skewer. Then push the air valve through the bung.

5 Choose your launch site carefully. (See the safety note above.)

6 Pour water into the bottle until it is about one third full. Push the bung tightly into the neck of the bottle and stand the rocket on its base. Attach the bicycle pump to the air valve, stand well to the side and start pumping.

◀ As you pump, you will see the bubbles of air rising through the water. The pressure builds up inside the bottle until the bung can no longer hold in place. Suddenly, the rocket blasts off, squirting out water as it lifts into the sky.

A windmill uses the force of the wind to do useful work. Water wheels turn the energy of running water into useful power. Before the first steam engines were invented, windmills and water wheels were almost the only machines that were not powered by human or animal muscles. Farmers often used them to grind corn and pump water.

MAKE it WORK!
Try making this simple windmill. The wind turns a crank, which makes a rod go up and down.

You will need

a wooden dowel	card
strong wood glue	wood
a sharp craft knife	a drill
strips of thin plastic	a cork
a tube of thick cardboard	wire and beads

1 Cut the four strips of wood to length to make the frame. Bend the wire crank to shape.

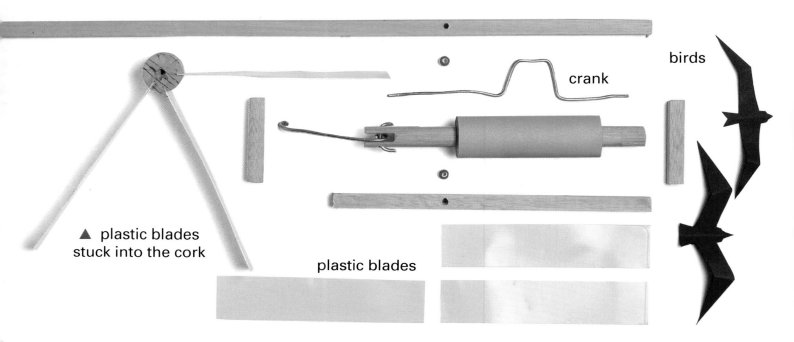

birds

crank

▲ plastic blades stuck into the cork

plastic blades

When engines fuelled by coal and oil came along, windmills and water wheels began to disappear. However, they are now becoming popular again. Today, we are more aware of the **pollution** caused by burning **fossil fuels** such as coal, gas and petrol. In comparison, wind and water power are clean and quiet sources of energy. They have another advantage too – unlike coal, gas and oil, our supplies of wind and water will never run out!

2 Drill holes facing each other in the longer frame side pieces to take the crank. Glue the frame together with the crank in place.

3 Ask an adult to help you cut slits in the cork. Slip the blades in place and secure with glue.

4 Slip a bead over each end of the crank shaft. Then push the cork onto one end of the shaft. Bend the other end to keep the shaft in place.

5 Cut a slot in one end of the dowel rod. Drill a hole at right angles to the slot and pass a small horseshoe-shaped wire through the hole.

6 Glue the cardboard tube to the top of the frame and push the dowel through it. Connect the wire horseshoe to the crank with a third piece of wire as shown. Make sure the dowel moves up and down easily as the crank turns.

7 Glue cardboard birds to the top of the dowel.

▶ Turn the mill by blowing a hair dryer at the blades. Experiment with the windmill out of doors too. Does it catch the wind better if you fit the blades into the cork at a different angle?

Modern windmills don't just grind corn or pump water. Nowadays, engineers can also build windmills to generate electricity.

Water power

Water wheels can be built wherever there is fast-flowing water that will turn the blades of the wheel. Most modern water wheels are complicated machines that are used to make electricity. They are called **hydroelectric turbines** and the electricity they produce is **hydroelectricity**. Hydroelectric turbines are usually built along big rivers or in dams, where water is made to pass through a turbine in order to get out of a reservoir. Electricity can even be generated in coastal areas, by the movement of the tides through a turbine.

▶ **Water wheel**
Try designing your own simple water wheel. This model has plastic blades fixed onto a cork, with a wooden dowel as an axle.

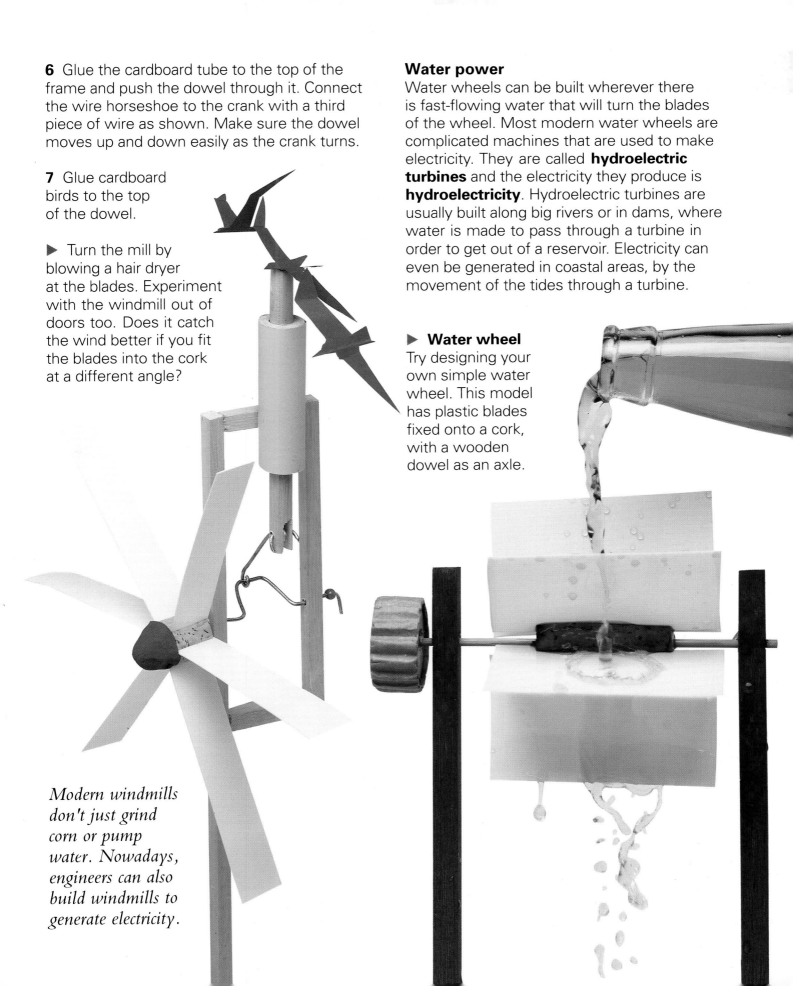

Rubber is an amazing material. You can stretch a rubber band to twice or three times its original length and it immediately springs back into shape when you let go. The stretched rubber stores energy. You can use this elastic energy to flick the band across the room, to make a catapult or even to power model cars, boats and planes.

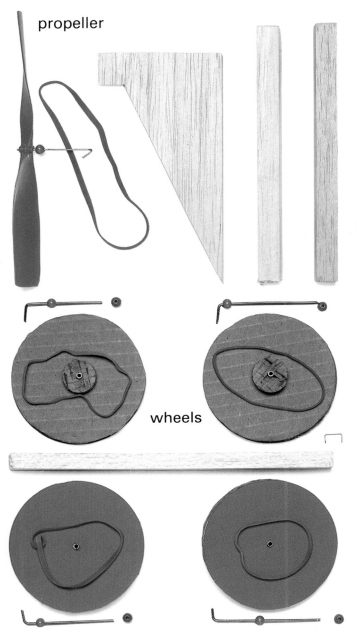

propeller

wheels

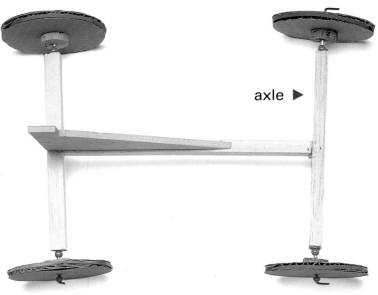

axle ▶

MAKE it WORK!

This roadster uses energy stored in a twisted rubber band to turn a propeller. The propeller pushes against the air, driving the car forwards.

You will need

balsa wood	beads
wire or thin nails	a cork
a model propeller	a stapler
thick rubber bands	a paperclip
thick corrugated card	a craft knife
very short pieces of thin metal tubing	

The roadster's cardboard wheels are quite difficult to make, but you could buy ready-made plastic wheels from a model shop.

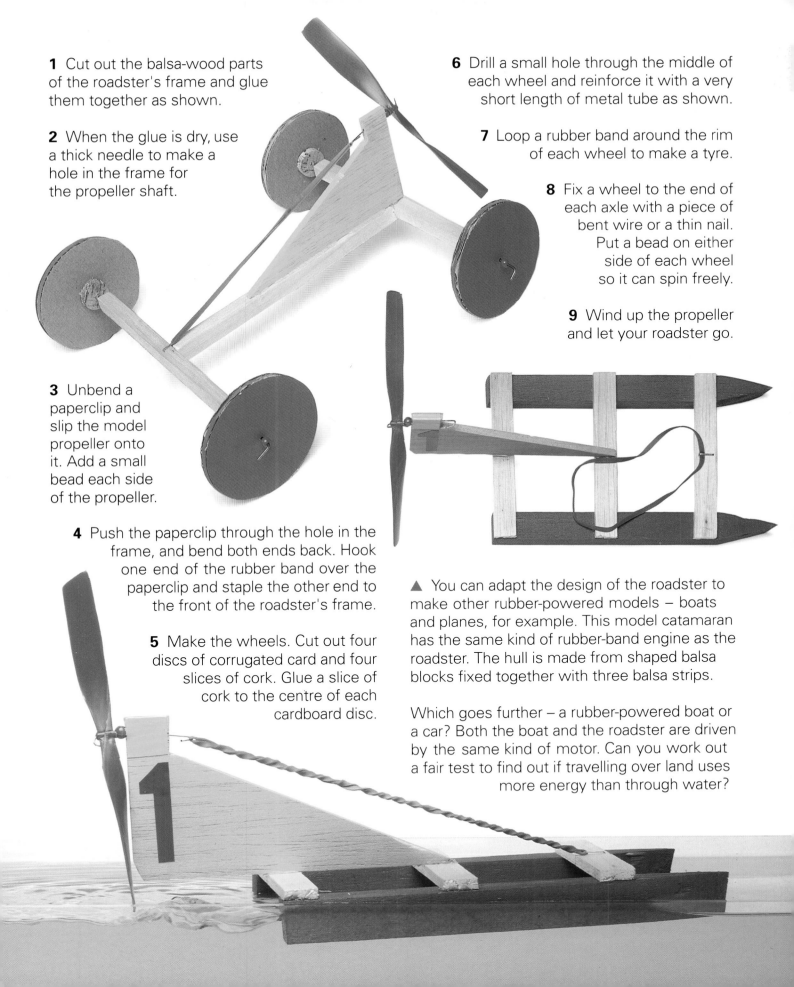

1 Cut out the balsa-wood parts of the roadster's frame and glue them together as shown.

2 When the glue is dry, use a thick needle to make a hole in the frame for the propeller shaft.

3 Unbend a paperclip and slip the model propeller onto it. Add a small bead each side of the propeller.

4 Push the paperclip through the hole in the frame, and bend both ends back. Hook one end of the rubber band over the paperclip and staple the other end to the front of the roadster's frame.

5 Make the wheels. Cut out four discs of corrugated card and four slices of cork. Glue a slice of cork to the centre of each cardboard disc.

6 Drill a small hole through the middle of each wheel and reinforce it with a very short length of metal tube as shown.

7 Loop a rubber band around the rim of each wheel to make a tyre.

8 Fix a wheel to the end of each axle with a piece of bent wire or a thin nail. Put a bead on either side of each wheel so it can spin freely.

9 Wind up the propeller and let your roadster go.

▲ You can adapt the design of the roadster to make other rubber-powered models – boats and planes, for example. This model catamaran has the same kind of rubber-band engine as the roadster. The hull is made from shaped balsa blocks fixed together with three balsa strips.

Which goes further – a rubber-powered boat or a car? Both the boat and the roadster are driven by the same kind of motor. Can you work out a fair test to find out if travelling over land uses more energy than through water?

For centuries, engineers dreamt of making machines that could fly like birds — but they didn't succeed until less than a hundred years ago. Because the pull of gravity is so strong and air is so thin, a plane can not get up off the ground unless it has a powerful engine **and** is very light for its size. A steam-powered plane carrying sacks of coal could never work!

You will need

a drill or bradawl	strong glue
a model propeller	a craft knife
thin card and balsa wood	a rubber band
two paperclips and a bead	wire and a cork

1 Cut the wing, tailplane and rudder from card.

2 Make the fuselage. Cut two strips of balsa wood 25 cm (10 in) long and two strips 5 cm (2 in) long. Glue them together as shown.

3 Use a thin drill or bradawl to make a small hole through each end of the fuselage.

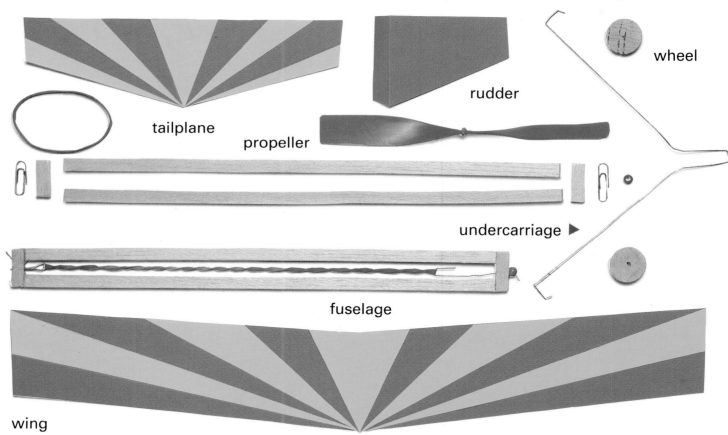

wheel

rudder

tailplane

propeller

undercarriage ▶

fuselage

wing

MAKE it WORK!

Rubber is light, so it makes a good engine for a model plane. This model stays in the air for just a few seconds, but you'll find it travels further than the roadster or the boat. Pushing through air is much easier than moving through water or rolling across the ground — so air travel can be more **efficient** than going by land or sea.

4 Make two hooks out of paperclips. Loop the rubber band over them and fit one hook in each hole in the fuselage as shown.

5 At the tail end, bend the hook right round and fix it firmly with tape so that it won't move. At the propeller end, add a bead, so that the hook can spin freely.

6 Attach the propeller and bend the paperclip hook round to hold it in place.

7 Glue the wings, tailplane and rudder in place.

8 Bend the wire to make the undercarriage shape and push on slices of cork to make wheels. Glue the wire onto the fuselage.

9 The plane is now complete – but before its first flight you must make sure that it balances properly. Rest the wing tips on your fingers. If it does not balance, add small pieces of Plasticine to the nose or the tail until it is level.

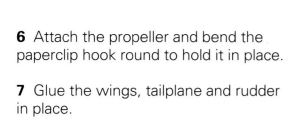

Test flight
Wind up the propeller until the band is twisted tightly. Hold the plane just behind the wing and launch it gently into the air.

If your plane nose dives, add more weight to the tail. If the plane stalls (the nose tips up and the plane slows down) add more weight to the nose.

Compared with petrol, rubber doesn't store much energy, so a rubber-band motor only powers short flights. But in 1979 one model flew for over 52 minutes – a world record!

When water boils it changes into steam. The steam needs more space than the water, so it pushes against the things around it. The inventor of the first steam engine probably saw steam pushing the lid up off a boiling kettle, and realized that this power could be used to push pistons and turn wheels.

MAKE it WORK!

These steam putt-putt boats are powered by a candle. The candle's flame boils water inside a thin metal tube. Puffs of steam squirt from one end of the tube and push the boat along. More cold water is then sucked back into the tube, to replace the steam that has been puffed out.

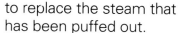

▲ Bending the metal tube

To make a putt-putt boat, you will need to twist a piece of brass or copper tubing. The easiest way to bend the tube is by winding it around a length of dowel. Make the bends slowly, taking care not to make kinks in the tube.

You will need

a cocktail stick   balsa wood
cardboard and glue   a wooden dowel
a small candle or night-light
a piece of soft brass or copper tubing
a length of bendy plastic pipe that will fit
  neatly over the metal tubing

1 Cut the balsa wood into the boat shape.

2 Twist the metal tube as shown above.

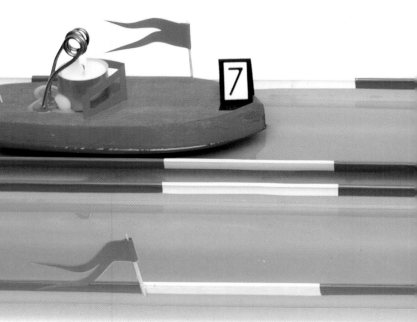

3 Ask an adult to help you push the two ends of metal tube through the balsa wood.

4 Cut the flag, windshield and number plate out of card, and fold and glue them in place. Then glue the candle on the boat as shown.

5 Push the plastic pipe over one end of the metal tube, and float the boat on the water.

6 Suck some water into the metal tube through the plastic pipe. When the tube is full, pull away the plastic, taking care not to lift the boat out of the water. Light the candle and watch your boat go!

The first steam engines did work that used to be done by horses, so an engine's strength was measured in horse power. A ten horse-power engine could do the work of ten horses. Today, even a small car engine has more than 50 horse power. But our putt-putt engine has only the power of a small insect!

▼ **Steam-boat race**
You could hold a race between two putt-putt boats along lengths of plastic guttering that are filled with water.

What would you call a machine that repeats the same movement, hour after hour? It's a clock! A clock moves in a very regular way, counting out the passing minutes as it goes.

MAKE it WORK!

Building a clock isn't easy – most machines tend to slow down or to get faster as they work. A machine that works steadily needs clever engineering to control the speed. Try it for yourself with this marble-operated clock!

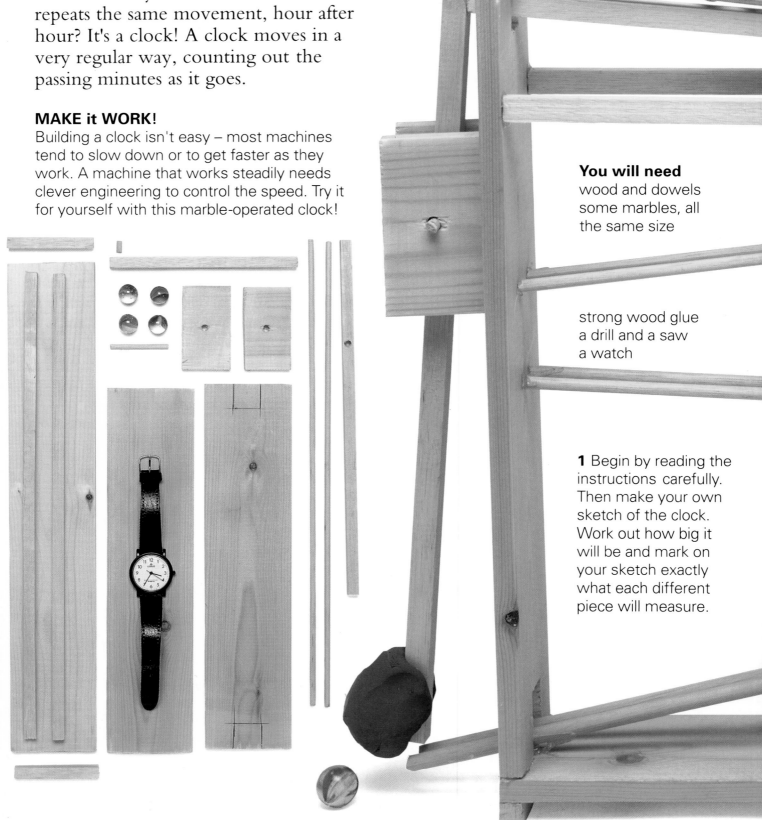

You will need
wood and dowels
some marbles, all
the same size

strong wood glue
a drill and a saw
a watch

1 Begin by reading the instructions carefully. Then make your own sketch of the clock. Work out how big it will be and mark on your sketch exactly what each different piece will measure.

2 Ask an adult to help you cut the pieces of wood needed to make the clock's frame. Cut a slot at the top and bottom of one side piece in the positions shown.

6 Cut two lengths of wood to make the lever arm. Drill a hole, a third of the way down the longer piece. Glue both pieces together as shown, adding a small wooden stop to the end of the shorter piece.

3 Firmly glue together the base, the side pieces and the two top crossbars.

7 Drill a hole in each of the lever supports and glue them to the frame. Fit the lever using a short dowel peg. Make sure the arm can swing freely.

4 Cut eight lengths of dowel to make slopes for the marbles to run down. Measure the dowels carefully, so that they are all slightly longer than the crossbars.

8 Start a marble on the run. At the bottom, it should knock the lever just hard enough to release the next marble.

5 Glue the slopes in place. Adjust them carefully, so that the gap between the two dowels is smaller at the top end and gets wider further down. At the bottom of each slope, the gap should be just wide enough for the marble to drop through and onto the slope below.

Use a watch with a second hand to time how long each marble takes to run from top to bottom.

Adjusting the lever
You'll probably need to adjust the lever to get it to work properly. If more than one marble is released at once, add a Plasticine weight to the bottom of the lever.

A modern electronic clock is very accurate and reliable. It will run for over a year on just one tiny battery and will lose or gain no more than a few seconds in that time. Early clocks were much cruder.

All the clocks on this page have been used in the past. How accurate do you think they are? Try making them and test them against your own watch.

Sand clocks

We still use sand clocks – sand running through an egg timer measures the minutes needed to cook a perfect boiled egg.

Make a cardboard funnel and fit it into the neck of a bottle. Fill the funnel with dry sand and see how long it takes to run through.

▶ Using a watch, make a scale on the sand clock. Mark the level of the sand at regular intervals (say every ten seconds). Are all of the marks evenly spaced? If not, why do you think the spacing changes?

Candle clocks

Monks in the Middle Ages often used candles to measure the time. With the help of an adult, test a candle yourself to see how far it burns in an hour. Make hour marks along the rest of the candle with tape. Then mark the half and quarter hours too. How accurate is this clock?

Water clocks

Do you ever lie awake at night listening to a dripping tap? The drips are sometimes so regular you can guess exactly when the next one is coming. The Ancient Chinese used dripping water to invent marvellous water clocks.

To make a water clock you will need

a glass
a straw
Plasticine
sticky tape
a large wooden bead
an old plastic container

1 Make a scale by marking the straw with tape. Fix the straw to the base of the glass with Plasticine.

2 Slip the bead over the straw.

3 Make a small hole in the bottom of the container. Then fill up the container with water and hold it over the glass.

4 As water drips into the glass, the bead rises up the scale. If the water runs too slowly, make a larger hole. If it is too quick, tape over the hole and make a smaller one.

More than three hundred years ago, the great Italian scientist, Galileo Galilei, sat in the cathedral at Pisa watching a hanging lantern swing to and fro. He realized that the lantern was a **pendulum**, *and that each of its swings took exactly the same amount of time.*

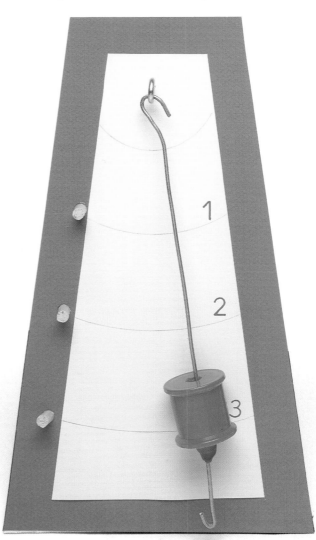

▲ Pendulum clock

A swinging pendulum is a good way of marking time. You can make a pendulum with a cotton reel, Plasticine and wire. Hang it from a hook and use your watch to investigate how the time taken by each swing changes as you move the reel up and down the wire.

Can you design any other machines of your own for measuring time?

Electricity

Scientists study the world around them and the way it works. They ask themselves questions and then work out systematic methods for answering those questions. Scientists usually start out with a **theory,** which they test by doing **experiments**. Then they observe and record the results.

Investigating electricity is part of the science of **physics**. Physicists study **energy** and **matter**, and find out how to put the forces of nature to work on our behalf. For instance, physicists discovered how to make **hydroelectricity** and **atomic** power.

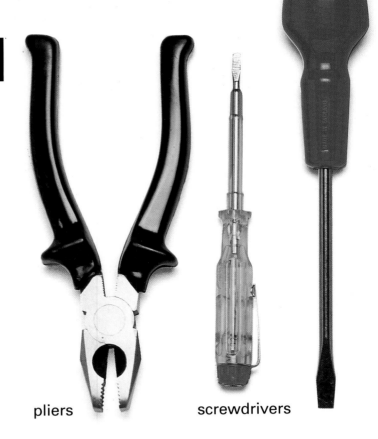

pliers   screwdrivers

MAKE it WORK!

This book is all about electricity. As you do the projects, you will be investigating the science of physics for yourself. It is important to use scientific methods. Draw pictures as accurately as you can, or take photographs. Write down clearly what you have done and observed.

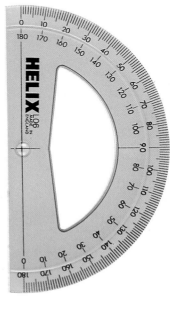

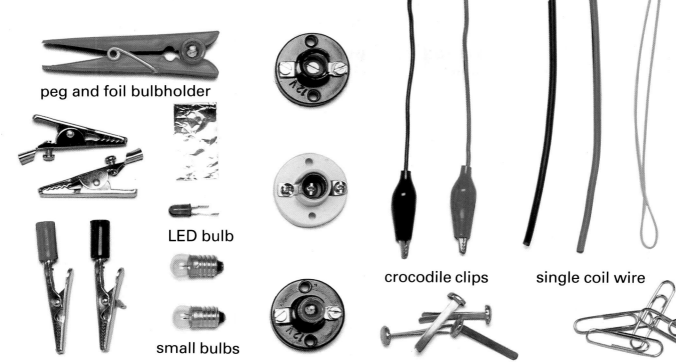

peg and foil bulbholder

LED bulb

small bulbs

crocodile clips

bulbholders

crocodile clips

single coil wire

paper fasteners

paper clips

electric motors

You will need

Notebooks, pens and pencils, tape, ruler, scissors and a protractor. Specialist equipment needed for the projects can be bought from any electrical goods or hobby shop.

Wire cutters and **pliers** Special wire cutters are best. You can use an old pair of scissors, but the wire will make them blunt.

Screwdrivers You will need a small, insulated electrical screwdriver and a larger one for screwing pieces of wood together.

Bulbs and bulbholders Use 6-volt bulbs and matching bulbholders. A square of tin foil held in place by a peg makes a good substitute bulbholder.

Wire Use single-core, plastic-coated wire.

Clips Buy crocodile clips for connecting wires to one another or to batteries. You can also use ordinary paper clips or paper fasteners.

Small electric motors These come from hobby shops in a variety of shapes and sizes. Use 3-volt or 6-volt motors.

Buzzers and **magnets** These are sold in model shops and hardware stores.

Batteries Most of the activities in this book use simple 6-volt or 4.5-volt flat batteries.
Be careful! Never touch car batteries and never plug anything into the mains sockets in your home. Mains electricity and large batteries are extremely dangerous!

horseshoe magnet

4.5-volt flat battery

Have you ever noticed that when you brush your hair, it sometimes sticks to the comb? That happens because of **static electricity**.

Every single thing is made up of tiny particles called **atoms**. Normally atoms have no electrical activity, but when two things rub together, like hair and a comb, the outer layer of **electrons** on the atoms of the hair are rubbed off. They stick to the atoms on the comb. When atoms lose electrons we say they become positively charged. When they gain electrons they are negatively charged. Two like charges repel one another – and different charges attract.

Repelling
Rub a balloon against your jumper and ask a friend to rub one too. Tie the balloons to a stick, with the rubbed sides facing each other. Because both balloons have the same charge, they swing away from one another.

MAKE it WORK!
With an **electroscope** you can test for the presence of static electricity.

You will need
bare wire
aluminium foil

a glass jar with a plastic lid
foil from a sweet wrapper
a plastic pen or ruler

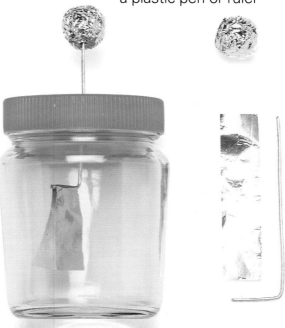

Ask an adult to help you push a piece of wire through the lid of a jam jar. Bend up one end and drape a thin piece of foil from a sweet wrapper over it. Crumple a ball of aluminium foil around the other end. Rub a plastic pen with a piece of silk or wool, and then hold it over the foil ball. If the pen is charged, then the sweet wrapper will move.

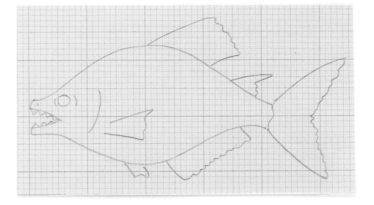

Attracting

Make some piranha fish like the ones above. Using the graph paper shape as a guide, cut out the fish from a single layer of coloured tissue paper. Place them on a flat surface. Rub a plastic ruler on a piece of silk or wool to get the ruler's electrons moving. Now pass the ruler over the fish and watch them jump up, attracted by the electric charge.

▼ Make some curly tissue-paper snakes and decorate them using stencils or felt-tip pens. (Be careful because tissue paper tears easily.) Pass a charged ruler over them – and watch them wiggle and wriggle!

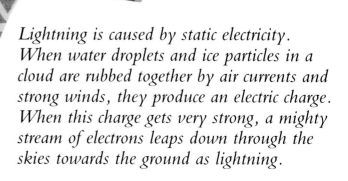

Lightning is caused by static electricity. When water droplets and ice particles in a cloud are rubbed together by air currents and strong winds, they produce an electric charge. When this charge gets very strong, a mighty stream of electrons leaps down through the skies towards the ground as lightning.

Static electricity itself is not very useful to us – we have to harness electricity before it can be used. The power that we actually use in our homes is called **current electricity** and is made up of millions of moving electrons.

An electric current is formed when the electrons in a substance, such as a piece of wire, are all made to move in the same direction. To provide us with electrical energy, the electrons must flow in an uninterrupted loop, called an electrical **circuit**.

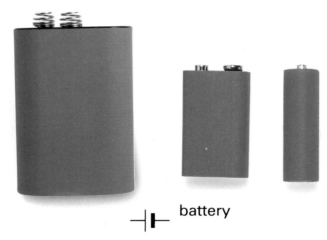

battery

▲ All the projects and activities in this book use batteries as the source of power.

bulbs   **bulbholder**

▲ Scientists and electrical engineers use special symbols when they are drawing or designing a circuit. This symbol is a bulb inside a bulbholder. A drawing of a whole circuit is called a circuit diagram.

MAKE it WORK!

Try making a simple circuit for yourself. It is very easy, but you must check carefully that all your connections are properly made.

You will need
a battery
wire
a bulb and bulbholder
paper clips/crocodile clips
a collection of household objects

1 Cut two pieces of wire about 15 cm (6 in) long. Strip the plastic coating from the ends of the wire, without breaking the wire itself.

2 Attach one piece of wire under each of the connecting screws on your bulbholder.

3 Attach the other ends of the wires to the battery **terminals**. If all your connections are made properly, the bulb should light up.

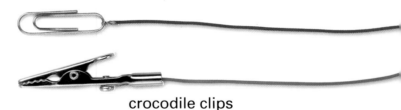

crocodile clips

*Anything that electricity can flow through, such as metal, is called a **conductor**. Materials, such as plastic, rubber and glass, that do not allow electricity to pass through them are called **insulators**. Electrical circuits make use of both conductors and insulators. The conductors, in this case the metal in the wires, allow the current to flow around the circuit. The insulators, such as the plastic around the wires and on bulbholders, stop the current from passing into any metal objects that the circuit is touching.*

▶ All circuits are made up of three basic elements: the conductor (the wire); the **load**, which uses the electricity (in this case a bulb); and the energy source (the battery).

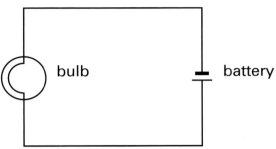

Conductor test

Test some household objects to see if they are conductors or insulators. Make a simple circuit with a gap in it, like the one below right. Touch an object with both wires. If the bulb lights up, you know that electricity must be passing through in order to complete the circuit. That means that the object must be a conductor.

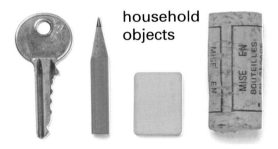

household objects

▶ Electrons flow through some materials better than others. The bulb shines brightly with a good conductor in the circuit and dimly with a poor one.

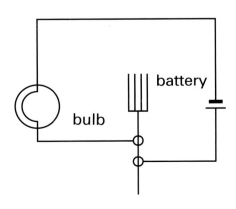

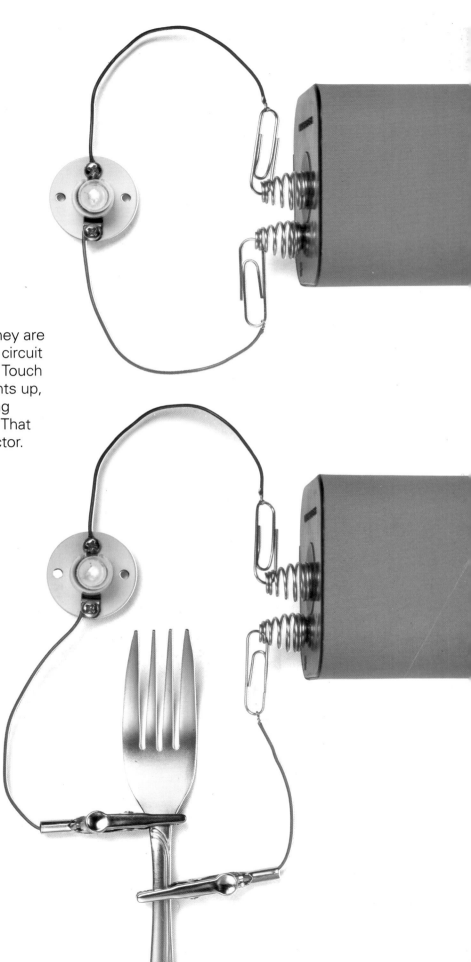

Batteries produce electricity from chemical energy. Usually, two metals, called electrodes, are placed in an **acid** solution called an **electrolyte**. A chemical reaction takes place and creates electric power.

MAKE it WORK!

There are many different kinds of battery. Wet batteries have metal plates in a liquid acid. In dry batteries, a chemical paste separates a carbon rod from the zinc case. Other batteries contain the metals nickel and cadmium, and an **alkaline** substance instead of an acid.

To make a wet battery you will need

a glass jar   white vinegar
wire   crocodile clips/paper clips
a strip of zinc   a piece of copper pipe
a light emitting diode (LED)

1 Put the strips of metal in the jar and fill it with vinegar. (Vinegar is a kind of acid.)

2 Attach clips and wires as shown, and the bulb will light up. However, LEDs only work when wired up the right way round. If yours doesn't light first time, reverse the connections.

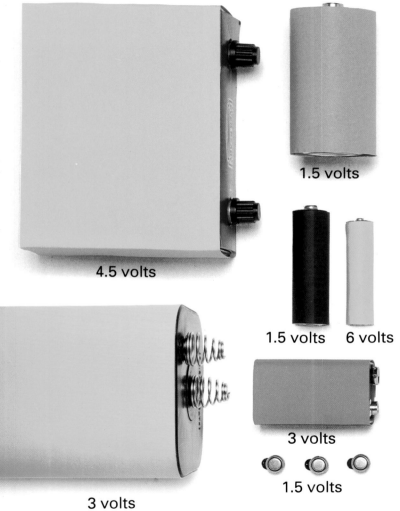

4.5 volts

1.5 volts

1.5 volts   6 volts

3 volts

1.5 volts

3 volts

Positive and negative

An electric current needs a destination in order to keep it moving. In a battery, two metals, zinc and copper, are used to make a current. When they are put into acid, negative electrons move from the copper to the zinc through the liquid. From the zinc, they move back down the wire to the copper, causing an electric flow.

The first battery was invented by an Italian count, Alessandro Volta, in the 1790s. It used silver and zinc discs, rather like our coin battery.

To make a battery tester you will need

balsa wood
insulated copper wire
screws and washers

card
a compass
wire and clips

1 Wrap the compass and the backing card in copper wire, attaching the ends to screws on the wooden base as shown.

2 To test a battery, clip wires from the battery terminals to the screws. The compass needle will move. Try this experiment with a brand new battery and a battery that has been used a lot. Can you notice a difference?

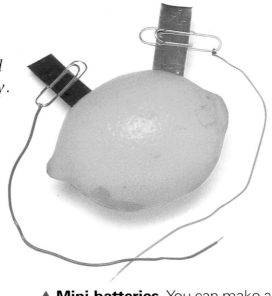

▲ **Mini-batteries** You can make a coin battery using silver and copper coins. Pair up the coins, and separate each pair with a square of blotting paper soaked in salty water. Attach a wire to the bottom coin of the pile, and a wire to the top coin. Don't let the wires touch each other, but clip them to your battery tester and see what happens. The current won't be very strong, but the tester should make some reaction.

You can also make a low-voltage mini-battery by pushing copper and zinc strips into a lemon.

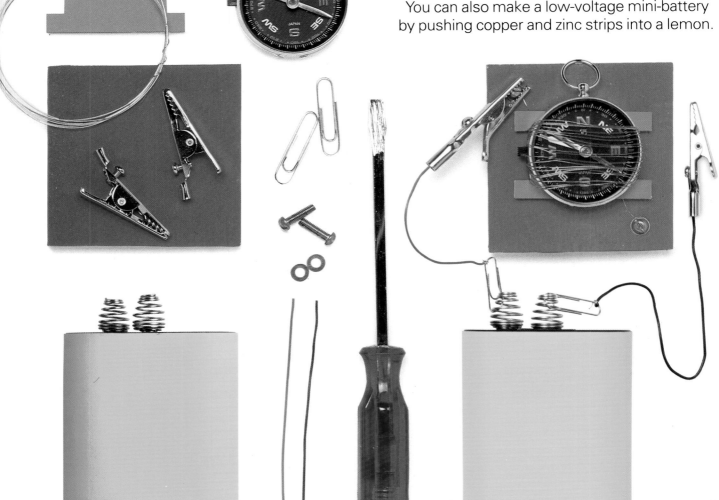

Electricity has many uses – in homes, factories and schools. It is produced in power stations by burning coal or oil fuels to power electricity **generators**. It can also be produced from nuclear fuel or in hydroelectric turbines.

MAKE it WORK!

Lighthouses were among the first users of electric power. Put your circuit-building know-how to good use and make a battery-operated mini-lighthouse for your bedroom.

You will need

thin card	glue and sticky tape
a craft knife/scissors	wire
a bulb and bulbholder	a battery
crocodile clips/paper clips	

1 Make a round tube from a piece of white card and decorate it with red stripes. You could also use the cardboard tube from a toilet roll and cover it with white paper.

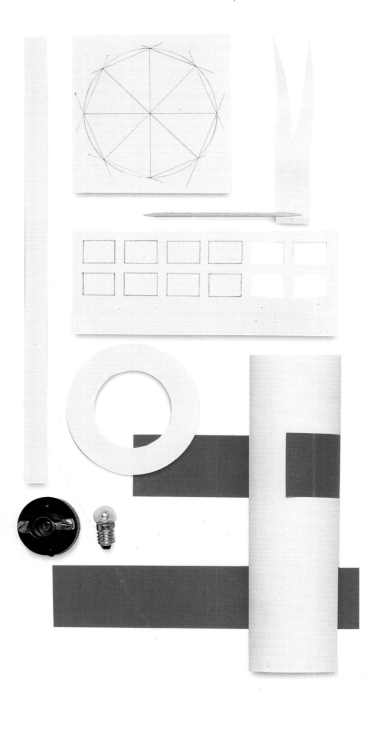

2 Cut out a circle of card for the balcony, make a hole in the centre, and glue or tape it to the top of the tube. Glue a strip of card around the edge of the balcony to make the rail.

3 Attach two long wires to a bulbholder and tape the bulbholder into place at the top of the tube. Push the wires down through the tube and out at the bottom.

4 Take a strip of card to make the windows at the top of the lighthouse. Cut out small squares with a craft knife or scissors, using the picture on the left as a guide. Then bend the card round to make a cylinder shape and glue it in position on the balcony.

5 To make the roof, draw a circle. Make two cuts close together from the rim to the centre and cut out a small segment. Fold and glue the circle to form a cone. Make a flag from paper and a cocktail stick.

6 Attach the ends of the wires to a battery and the bulb in your lighthouse will light up.

The first people to build lighthouses were probably the Ancient Egyptians. They began by lighting bonfires on hilltops to guide their ships. During the third century BC, they built the tallest ever lighthouse, the Pharos of Alexandria, which was over 122m (400 ft) high.

Scientists measure electricity with two separate units called volts and watts. Volts measure electrical force, the amount of power produced by a source of electricity, such as a battery. Watts measure the electrical power at the point where it is actually used – in an electric fire or bulb, for instance.

▲ To hide the battery that operates your lighthouse, make a 'rock' out of pieces of old cardboard, stuck together in a jagged shape and painted. Around the lighthouse, put a series of buoys like those on the next page.

In an electrical circuit, all the parts must be joined up to one another, so that the current can flow. There are basically two ways of wiring a circuit with more than one **component** (or part) – in series or in parallel.

MAKE it WORK!

In a series circuit, the electric current flows along a single path, going through each of the components in turn. If one component is removed, or breaks (when the filament in a bulb burns out, for instance), all the other components will stop working too.

In a parallel circuit, each of the components is connected to the battery on its own branch of the main circuit. Even if one of the bulbs in a parallel circuit burns out, the other bulbs will continue to shine, because their own branches of the circuit remain complete.

You will need

card or thick paper	scissors/a craft knife
wire	glue and sticky tape
batteries	bulbs and bulbholders
crocodile clips/paper clips	

1 You are going to make a string of buoys like the ones used to mark out shipping lanes. For each buoy you will need to cut out the shapes you see below from thin card: a semicircle for the body, a strip with windows for the lantern and a circle with a slit in it for the cone-shaped top. Use a craft knife to cut out the windows.

2 Assemble the buoys as shown below, fitting a bulbholder firmly into the body of each buoy with sticky tape.

3 Wire up the series circuit as shown on the left-hand side of the opposite page. Take a wire from bulbholder to bulbholder, completing the circuit from the last buoy back to the battery. You could put a switch in this section if you wish to.

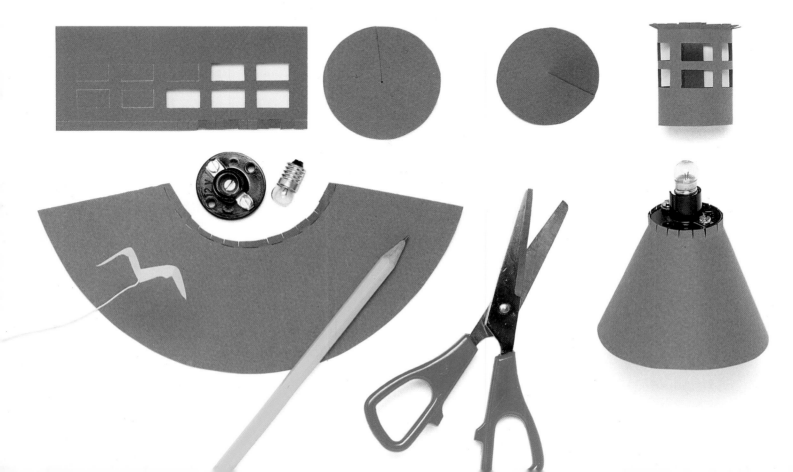

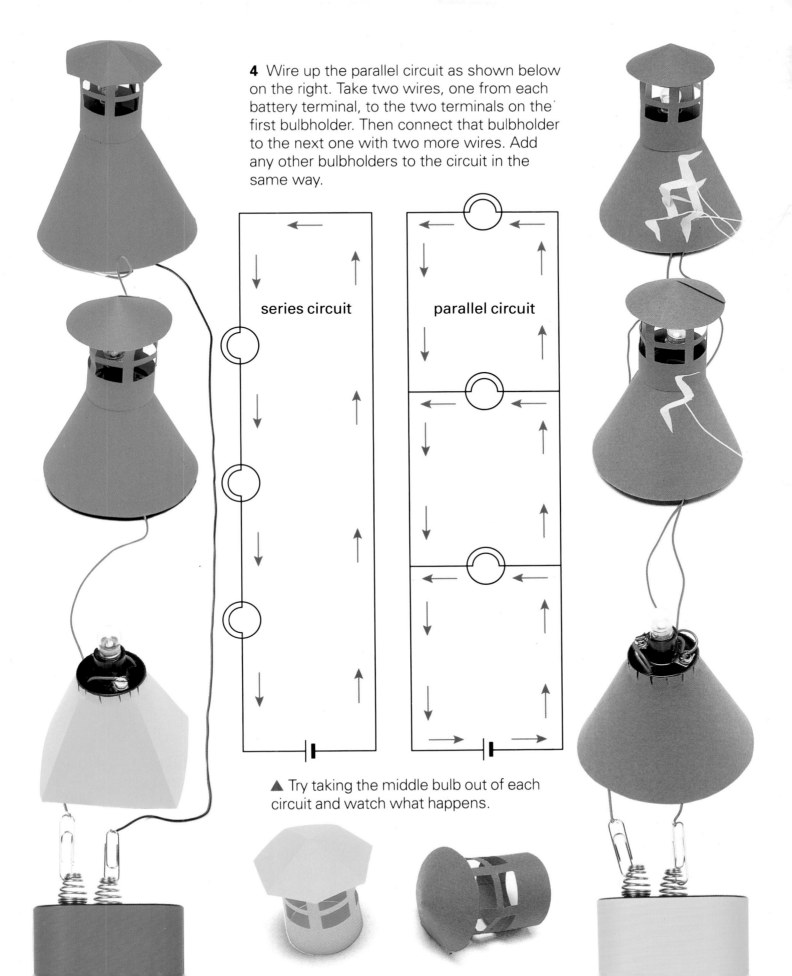

4 Wire up the parallel circuit as shown below on the right. Take two wires, one from each battery terminal, to the two terminals on the first bulbholder. Then connect that bulbholder to the next one with two more wires. Add any other bulbholders to the circuit in the same way.

series circuit

parallel circuit

▲ Try taking the middle bulb out of each circuit and watch what happens.

Light bulbs are used to produce light from electricity. The bulb contains a thin metal thread called a **filament**. When an electric current forces its way through this thin part of the circuit, the filament glows a bright white colour and the bulb gives off light.

You will need
a collection of old light bulbs
a craft knife
glue or tape
card
a ruler

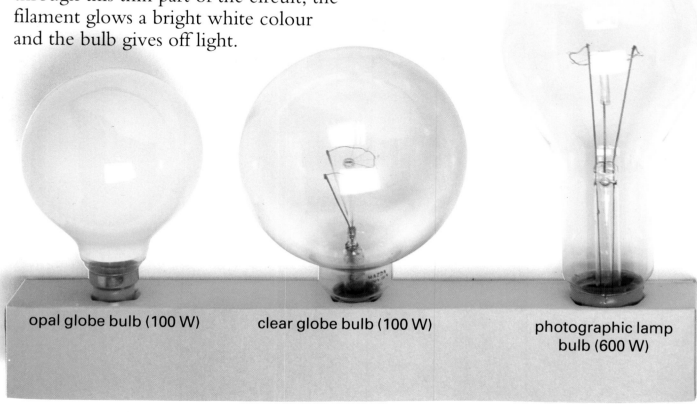

opal globe bulb (100 W)   clear globe bulb (100 W)   photographic lamp bulb (600 W)

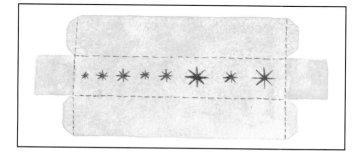

MAKE it WORK!

Light bulbs come in all shapes and sizes. Make a collection of different light bulbs, with a special box to display and store your collection. New bulbs are expensive, so just collect those which do not work any more. Handle light bulbs carefully, as the glass is delicate.

1 Work out what size you want your box. Then cut out a flat shape like the one on the left.

2 Fold up the sides of the box. Tuck in the corner flaps and glue or tape them in place.

3 Carefully cut the card along the top of the box so that you make spaces where you can stick the ends of the bulbs. Make sure that the bulbs fit in firmly.

4 Try to label your collection. Mark the different types of bulb (whether they have a filament or a fluorescent tube) and also how bright they are. You can tell the brightness of a bulb from the number of watts (W) of power that it uses.

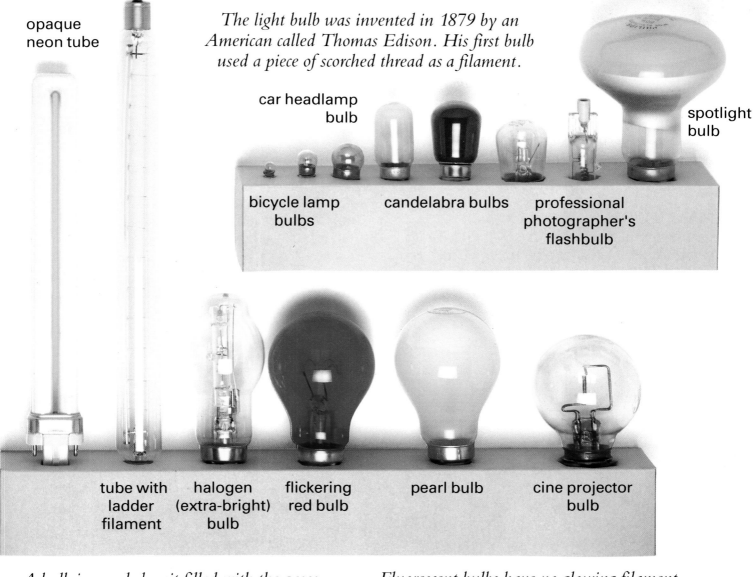

opaque
neon tube

*The light bulb was invented in 1879 by an
American called Thomas Edison. His first bulb
used a piece of scorched thread as a filament.*

car headlamp
bulb

spotlight
bulb

bicycle lamp
bulbs

candelabra bulbs

professional
photographer's
flashbulb

tube with
ladder
filament

halogen
(extra-bright)
bulb

flickering
red bulb

pearl bulb

cine projector
bulb

*A bulb is a sealed unit filled with the gases
nitrogen or argon. It contains no oxygen, the
gas in the air that substances need to burn.
Nitrogen or argon lets the filament glow,
but doesn't allow it to catch fire.*

*Fluorescent bulbs have no glowing filament.
Electricity is passed through a gas contained
under pressure in the   bulb. The gas gives
off light, but the bulbs   don't get very hot.*

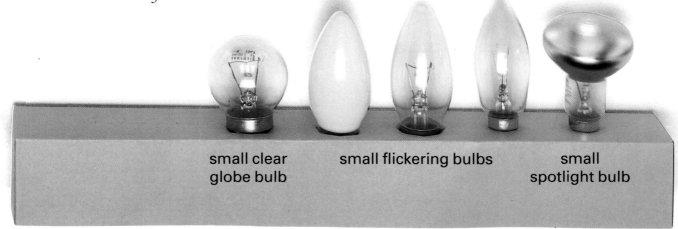

small clear
globe bulb

small flickering bulbs

small
spotlight bulb

An electric current must always flow through a complete circuit. No current can flow in a broken circuit, because electrons have to keep moving in a continuous stream.

MAKE it WORK!

Test how steady your hand is with this circuit game. At the start of the game, the circuit is broken, so the light is off. If your hand shakes as you move the playing stick along, the loop touches the wire, the circuit is completed and the bulb lights up!

You will need

a battery	wire
a bulb and bulbholder	dowel
crocodile clips/paper clips	coloured tape
an old wire coathanger	
screw eyes, large and small	
balsa wood and wood glue, or a shoe box	

Most coathangers are lacquered with a thin layer of clear plastic to stop them marking cloth. You should rub away the plastic with a piece of sandpaper – otherwise the plastic will insulate the wire and the circuit won't work.

1 Make the playing stick by screwing a large screw eye into the end of the dowel. Connect a long piece of wire to the eye, and tape it down the length of the playing stick.

2 Make a box by gluing together pieces of wood, or use a shoe box. Paint the box, then divide it into sections with coloured tape.

3 Position the bulbholder at one end of the box, wire it up and push the wires through the top of the box.

screw eye　　　　　　**dowel**

wire

4 Twist a small screw eye onto each end of the box. If you are using a shoe box, you may have to tape them in place. Bend and twist the coathanger wire to make the top part of the game. Slip the eye on the handle over the wire. Then connect the ends of the coathanger wire to the screw eyes on the box.

5 Beneath the box, connect one of the wires from the bulbholder to the battery. Put a crocodile clip on the other bulbholder wire and attach it to one end of the bent coathanger.

6 Connect the wire from the playing stick to the free battery terminal. Now you are ready to play the game!

circuit diagram of the circuit game

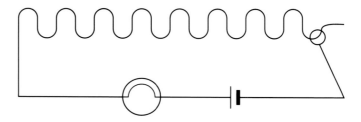

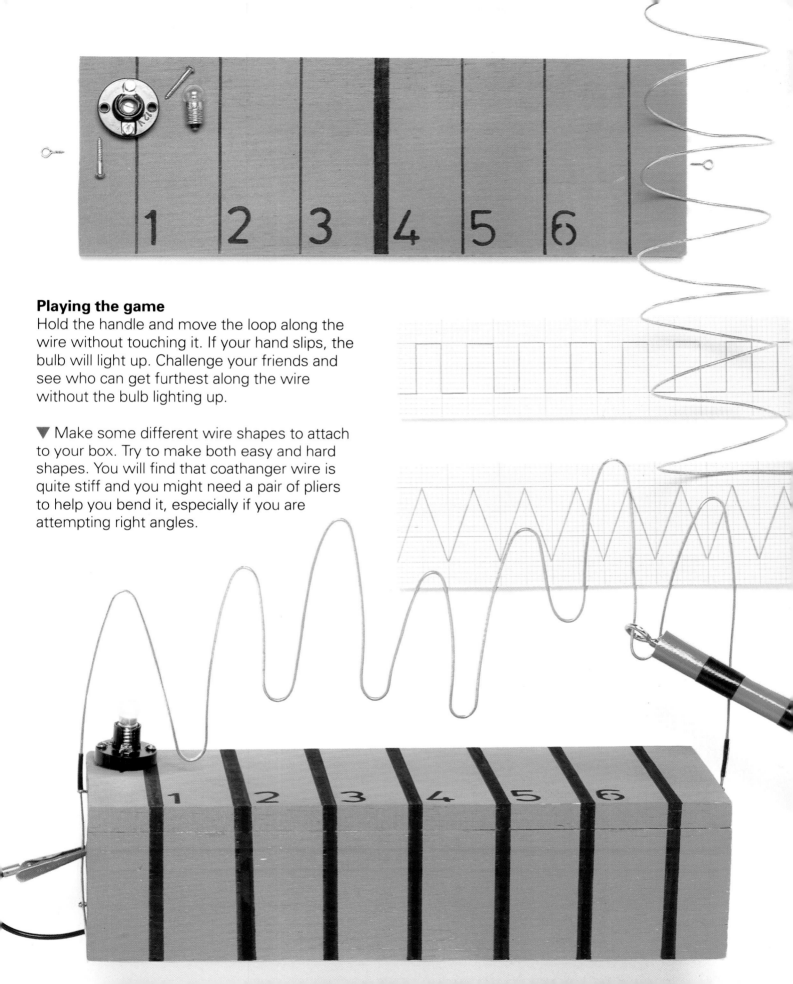

Playing the game

Hold the handle and move the loop along the wire without touching it. If your hand slips, the bulb will light up. Challenge your friends and see who can get furthest along the wire without the bulb lighting up.

▼ Make some different wire shapes to attach to your box. Try to make both easy and hard shapes. You will find that coathanger wire is quite stiff and you might need a pair of pliers to help you bend it, especially if you are attempting right angles.

Switches are used to turn electrical circuits on and off. When they are switched off, they break the circuit so that electricity cannot flow around it. When they are switched on, they complete the circuit, allowing the electricity to flow through.

MAKE it WORK!

Switches can be made to work in lots of different ways. For instance, you may not want a light to go out completely, but just to be a little less bright. Or you may need a switch that can turn a buzzer on and off very quickly, to make a special pattern of signals. Here are four different types of switch for you to try.

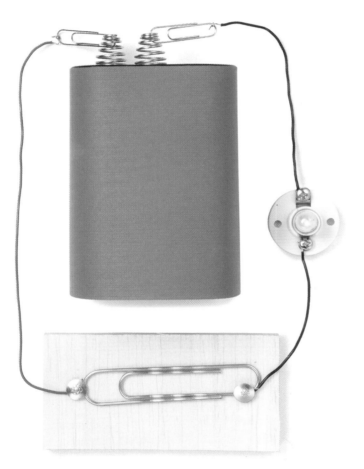

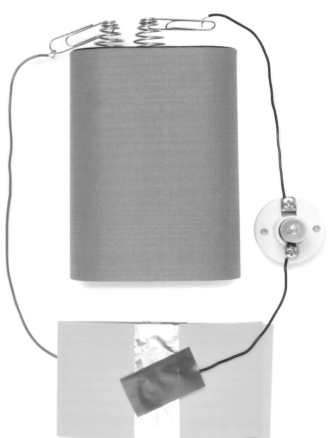

Simple switch

This is a simple on/off switch. When it is on, the current flows through the circuit; when it is off, the current stops. Wire up a simple circuit, like the one on page 8, but leave a break in the wires. Make a switch as shown above, using a block of balsa wood, a paper clip and two metal drawing pins. When the clip touches both drawing pins, the switch is on.

Pressure switch

This is the type of switch that can be used to make a doorbell ring when someone steps on a doormat. Wire up a circuit as before. Fold a piece of card in half. Wrap strips of foil around each half of the card, so that they touch when pressed together. Tape the wires to the foil on the outside of each side of the card. When the two strips of foil touch, the switch is on.

These are low-voltage switches from a model shop. You can include them in any of the circuits shown in this book.

You will need

batteries	wire
bulbholders	bulbs
balsa wood	card
paper clips	tape
drawing pins	cork
aluminium foil	a pencil
strips of thin copper	a crocodile clip

Dimmer switch

Electricity can pass through the **graphite** in a pencil, but it is hard work. Graphite is called a **resistor,** because it offers resistance to the electric current. You can use a graphite pencil resistor to make a dimmer switch. The longer your pencil lead, the more resistance there is and the dimmer your light will be.

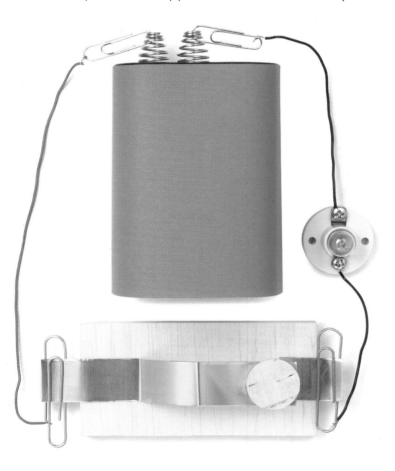

Tapper switch

This switch is used by Morse code operators. It gives the operator total control over the length of time the circuit is complete or broken. The switch is on when the two strips of copper are pressed together. It returns automatically to the 'off' position when not in use. The full instructions for how to make a Morse code tapper are given over the page.

Make a simple circuit as before, but fit crocodile clips to the free ends of the wire. Soak a lead pencil in water, and then ask an adult to slice it open down the middle. (**Be careful!** You should not try to cut the pencil yourself.) Attach the crocodile clips to opposite ends of the pencil lead, and then gradually slide one clip towards the other. What happens?

Morse code was invented in 1840 by the American painter and inventor, Samuel Morse. Each letter of the alphabet is represented by a simple combination of short and long electrical signals which can easily be transmitted down a single wire. The code is written down on paper as dots, dashes and spaces. Before the days of **communications satellites** and fax machines, all international newspaper reports and messages were sent flashing and buzzing down telegraph wires by Morse code operators.

MAKE it WORK!
Make a pair of Morse code tappers for sending and receiving secret messages.

You will need
two pieces of wood	two batteries
two bulbs and bulbholders	wire
two strips of copper	paper clips
two slices of cork	glue and screws

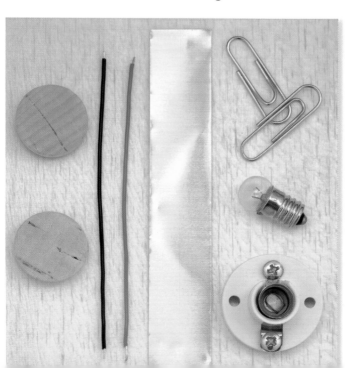

▼ International Morse code
These are the Morse code symbols. As you can see, they are made up of dots, dashes and spaces. A dot is transmitted by pressing and instantly releasing the transmitter key. To send a dash, hold the key down twice as long as you did for the dot. A space between letters is the same length as a dot, and a space between words is the same length as a dash.

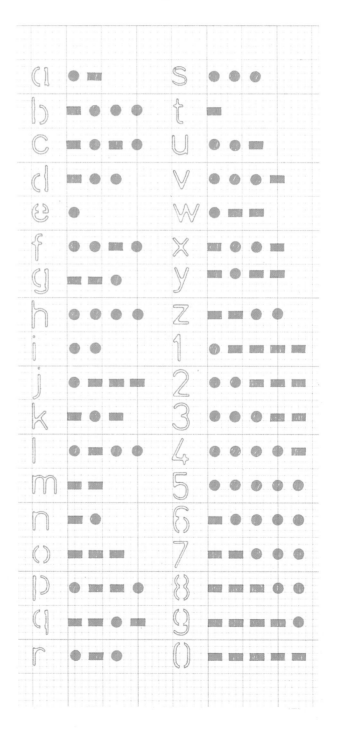

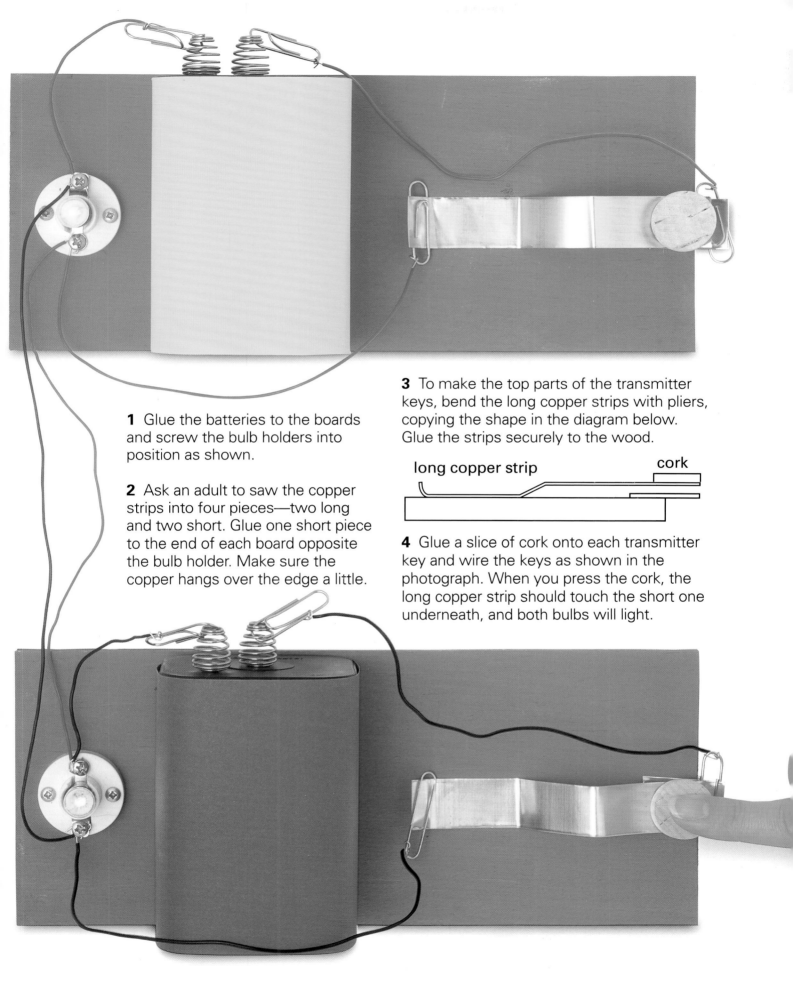

1 Glue the batteries to the boards and screw the bulb holders into position as shown.

2 Ask an adult to saw the copper strips into four pieces—two long and two short. Glue one short piece to the end of each board opposite the bulb holder. Make sure the copper hangs over the edge a little.

3 To make the top parts of the transmitter keys, bend the long copper strips with pliers, copying the shape in the diagram below. Glue the strips securely to the wood.

long copper strip   cork

4 Glue a slice of cork onto each transmitter key and wire the keys as shown in the photograph. When you press the cork, the long copper strip should touch the short one underneath, and both bulbs will light.

Some circuits are made up of lots of different connections, which act together to perform complex tasks. In electrical equipment such as radios, where many tiny circuits are needed, the circuits themselves may not be made as wires, but tiny strips of metal printed on a sheet. In computers, thousands of microscopic circuits are crammed onto one **silicon chip**.

MAKE it WORK!

Most circuits are made on a circuit board. All the wires are spaced out so they cannot accidentally touch one another. This question and answer game shows you what a simple circuit board looks like. Each connection, when correctly made, will complete a circuit and the bulb will light up.

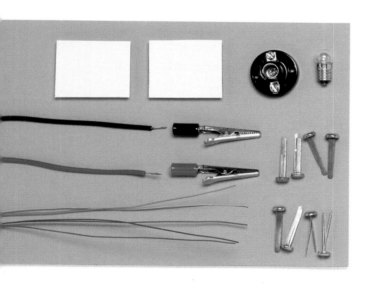

You will need

wire	card
a battery	paper fasteners
a bulb and bulbholder	a buzzer
stick-on Velcro tape	coloured pens
crocodile clips/paper clips	

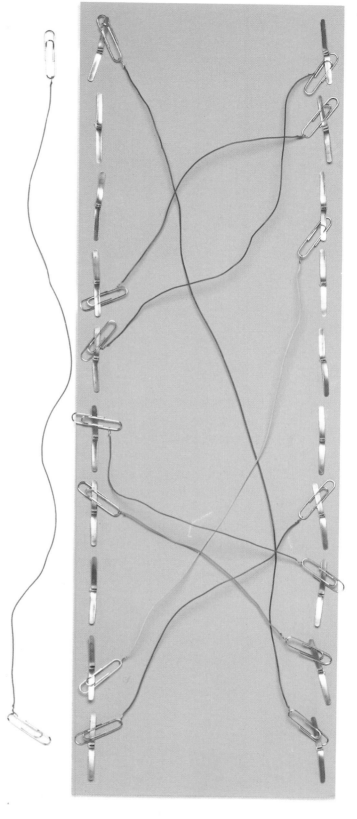

1 Cut out a piece of card for your quiz board. Down each side of the card, push through a row of paper fasteners. On the front of the card, stick strips of Velcro backing tape next to each paper fastener.

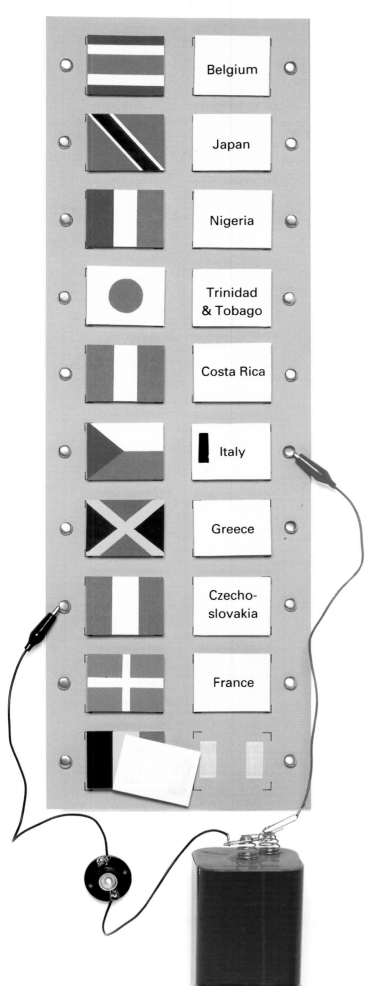

2 Make question and answer cards. Back them with Velcro and stick them down in random order. On the back of the board, wire up the questions to the correct answers.

3 Set up your testing kit of battery, bulb, wires and clips as shown.

4 Touch one of the paper fasteners on the question side with one of the testing wires. Then match it up with an answer on the other side. If you have picked the correct answer, the electrical circuit will be completed and the bulb will light up.

▲ Make raised shapes for your quiz board and replace the light bulb with a buzzer. Now you can play blindfold!

▲ ▼ Think up different quizzes for your board. What about animals, or tennis players?

Always check your connections carefully before you start to play. The game will not work if any of the wires become loose.

Just like static electricity, magnetism is a natural, invisible force. It was discovered over 2,000 years ago, when the Ancient Greeks first noticed that certain stones would jump together or move apart depending on which way they were facing.

What is a magnet?
A magnet is a piece of iron or steel that attracts or repels certain other pieces of iron or steel. Like all other substances, metals are made up of the tiny particles we call **molecules** which, in turn, are made up of atoms. Normally, all the molecules in a piece of iron are facing in different directions. However, if we can rearrange the molecules and get them all facing the same way, they will act together as a magnet, making a powerful force.

MAKE it WORK!
You can watch the power of magnets at work with this fishing game. The object is to 'catch' as many high-scoring fish as possible. Players take it in turns to fish, and the winner is the player with the highest score.

1 Using the shape above, cut out large, medium and small versions of the fish from different colours of card.

2 Draw in the eye, gill and mouth using a thick black marker.

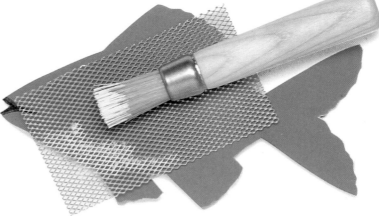

3 To get a fish-scale effect, stipple paint onto the fish using a stencil brush and a piece of wire mesh. Use a lighter coloured paint on the belly. Give each fish a score number.

You will need

thin card   paint and paint brushes
thin wire mesh   dowels and string
a craft knife   paper clips
a small magnet with a hole in the centre

4 Make fishing lines by tying the magnet to the string. Attach the other end of the string to a dowel rod as shown.

5 Attach paper clips to the fishes' noses.

6 Make a sea from a cardboard box covered in blue card. Put in the fish and start fishing.

Around a magnet is an area called a **force field**, where the pull or push of metal and magnet is at its strongest. The force field is strong enough to pass through wood or glass. The ends of a magnet, where most of the energy is directed, are much more powerful than the middle.

MAKE it WORK!

The more powerful the magnet, the larger and stronger its force field. See how a small magnet works through card, and how the force field of a strong steel magnet can even pass through a wooden door.

For the insects you will need

card	glue
slices of cork	paint and paint brushes
metal drawing pins	a horseshoe magnet

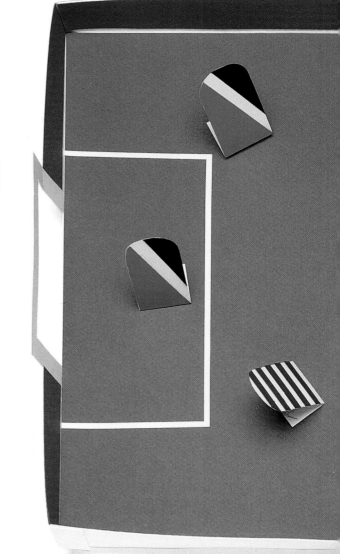

Magnetic insects

Using a craft knife, cut out insect shapes from thin card and paint them carefully. Stick each insect onto a small square of cork into which you have pushed a drawing pin. Use a strong horseshoe magnet to make the insects move from the other side of a door.

For the football game you will need

white card	green card
a craft knife	cork
metal drawing pins	dowels
small magnets	glue
a table football ball	paints or crayons

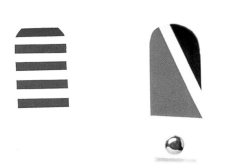

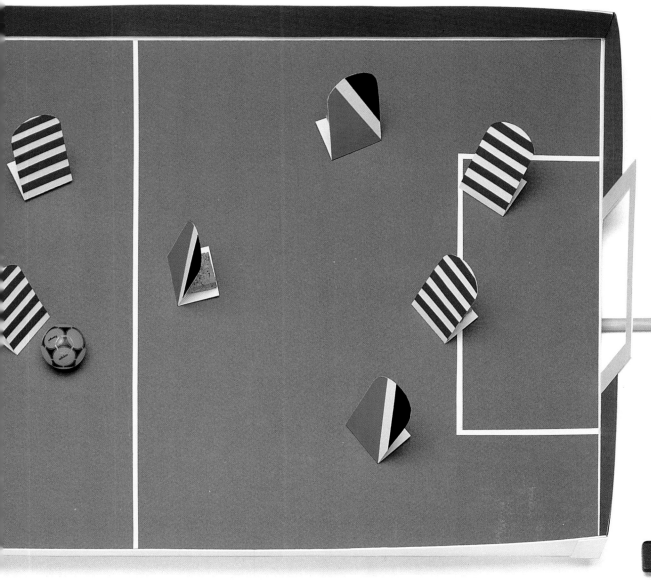

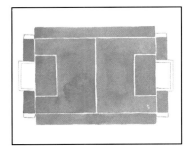

Table football

Make a box out of green card, folding and gluing the corners as shown. Mark out the lines of the football pitch in white. Make cardboard players with a piece of cork glued to the inside of each base. Stick a drawing pin through from the outside. The players are moved from under the pitch by magnets attached to dowels.

The force fields of magnets can pass through many different substances. The magnetic insects and magnetic football on the previous pages work because magnets can attract through wood and cardboard. A magnetic force field can also pass through water.

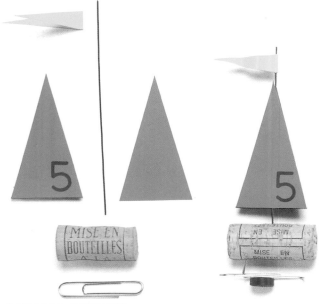

MAKE it WORK!

There are two different kinds of magnetic boat to make. The cork boats work by magnet to magnet attraction. The boat magnets are close to the bottom of the water container, so the boats can be pulled around by a small bar magnet attached to the end of a stick. The balsa-wood boat has drawing pins pushed into its keel and needs a stronger magnet with a force field that will attract through shallow water.

Even though the Ancient Greeks knew of magnets, for hundreds of years people did not know how to make magnets for themselves. It was not until the nineteenth century that magnetism, and its close connection to electricity, were properly understood.

You will need

thin, coloured card	wire
corks	paper clips
door magnets	glue
dowels	strong magnets
balsa wood	a wooden skewer
metal drawing pins	a glass tank

To make the cork boats

1 Make the sails out of coloured card. You can make one triangular sail by cutting out two triangles and sticking them back to back with the mast in the middle.

2 You can also make a more complex rig of a mainsail and jib. Cut a rectangle of card diagonally, leaving enough card on the straight edge to make two tabs. With these tabs, attach the sail to a piece of wire.

3 Push the wire mast into a cork. **Be very careful!** Do not stab yourself with the wire. Top the mast with a flag made from a folded strip of card of a contrasting colour.

4 Unbend a paper clip as shown above. Push one end into the underside of the cork and glue a small door magnet onto the other end, using waterproof glue.

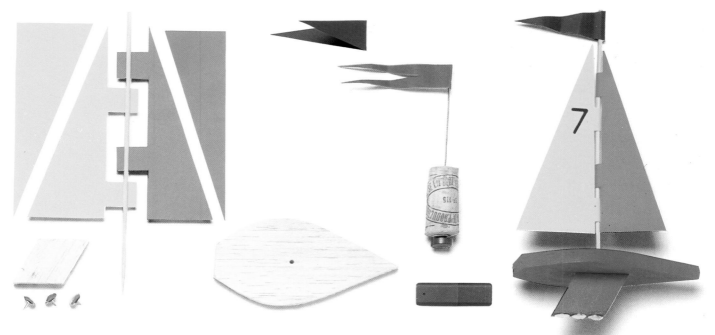

To make the balsa-wood boat

1 Ask an adult to help you cut a deck and keel out of balsa wood as shown above.

2 Stick a wooden skewer into the centre of the deck to make a mast.

3 Make sails and flags as for the cork boats, but in a larger size.

4 Glue the boat together with waterproof glue and paint it. Push three drawing pins into the bottom of the keel.

To make the buoys

Put a short piece of wire into a cork and top it with a coloured flag. Stick a door magnet to the bottom of the cork with waterproof glue.

The Ancient Greeks had a mythical story about an island of magnetic mountains, which pulled the iron nails out of passing ships!

The Earth itself is a giant magnet and, like any other magnet, its strongest points are at the North Pole and the South Pole. No one really knows why the Earth is a magnet, but its force field extends thousands of miles into space. Any magnet on Earth allowed to swing freely will always point to the north – which is very handy if you need to find out where you are.

1 Cut out a circle of card and make a hole in the centre just smaller than the diameter of the yoghurt pot.

2 Using a protractor, divide the circle into accurate quarters and mark on the four compass points: north, south, east and west.

3 Make the needle magnetic by stroking it with one end of a magnet about twenty times. Always stroke in the same direction. Tape the needle onto a thin slice of cork.

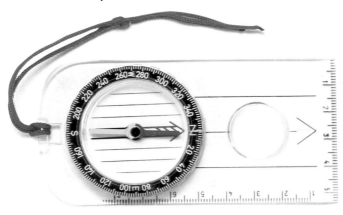

MAKE it WORK!

Because magnets always line up with magnet Earth, the end of a magnet that points north is called the north pole and the end that points to the south is called the south pole. Compasses are used to find directions, and they come in many varieties. Some are marked off with all 180 degrees of a circle. These compasses give a very accurate reading, but even the simplest compass will let you know if you are heading in the right direction. All you need is a magnetized needle that can swing freely.

To make a water compass you will need

an old yoghurt pot	a magnet
a needle	a slice of cork
card	a protractor

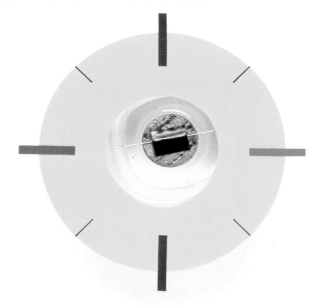

4 Fill the yoghurt pot with water and float the cork in it. When the needle has settled to the north, tape the ring of card onto the pot. Check your readings against a real compass.

The poles of magnets react to one another just like the two kinds of electric charge. Opposite poles attract – and like poles repel.

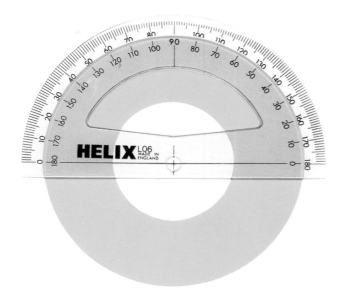

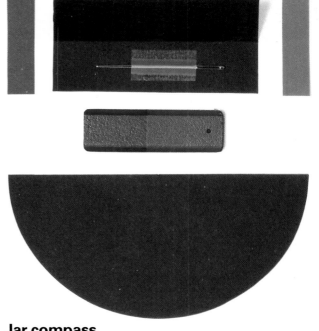

For two simple compasses you will need

card   needles
a magnet   tape

Fold a strip of card and tape a magnetized needle on it.

Jar compass
Suspend the compass strip in a glass jar using a straw or a pencil and some thread. This compass will work out of doors because the jar protects the needle from the wind.

◀ Balancing compass
Make a cone from a semicircle of card. Fix a wooden skewer or cocktail stick into the top of the cone and balance the compass strip on the end. This is strictly an indoor model!

You can actually see the force field that surrounds a magnet by sprinkling iron filings onto a piece of paper and then putting a magnet wrapped in paper down amongst them. The filings will rearrange themselves according to the magnet's force field, clustering around the north and south poles where the force is at its greatest.

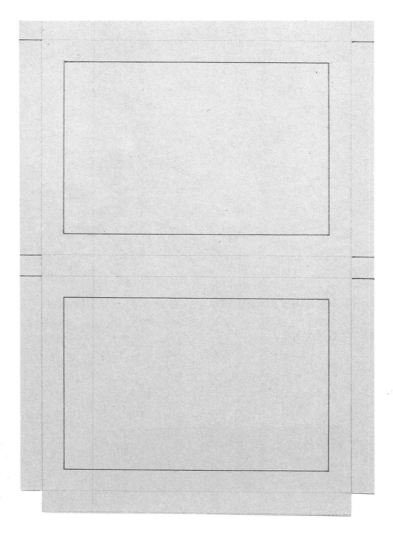

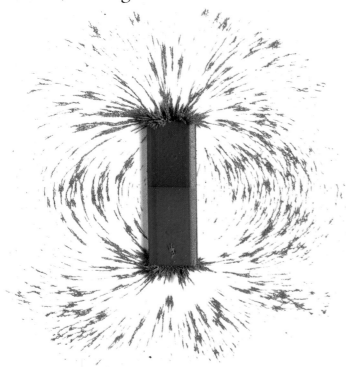

▲ Here you can see the force field at work. The iron filings form a pattern of lines running from pole to pole. These lines are called lines of force, and they show up the invisible force field of the magnet.

Be careful! Iron filings are dangerous. Don't breathe them in or swallow any, and don't lick your fingers after touching them.

MAKE it WORK!
Use the power of magnetism to draw pictures with iron filings.

You will need
card	clear acetate sheets
rubber bands	iron filings and a magnet
scissors	clear sticky tape

1 Cut out a rectangle of card and mark it as shown. Cut along the red lines and fold and glue along the pencil lines to make a box.

2 Take two pieces of clear acetate and cut them slightly bigger than the windows of the drawing box. Tape them in place with clear sticky tape.

3 Draw some faces on sheets of white card, leaving out the hair.

4 Put a face card inside the box and shake iron filings on top of the card. Snap the box shut with the elastic bands. Put the drawing box on a flat surface. Now you can 'draw' the hair on your face using a magnet.

A new kind of experimental train in Japan runs on the principle of magnetic levitation. Both the track and parts of the train are magnetic. It works on the pull and push of magnets that repel and attract. The train floats above the track because the train and the track repel one another. There are no wheels and tracks to wear out, and no **friction** *to slow the train down.*

We have seen that electricity and magnetism are closely related to each other. In fact, every electric current has its own magnetic field. This magnetic force in electricity is very handy. We can use electricity to make powerful **electromagnets** that can be turned on and off at the flick of a switch.

MAKE it WORK!

This crane uses an electromagnetic coil. The magnetic field produced by a single wire is not very strong, but when electricity flows through a wire coiled around a nail, the coil becomes a powerful magnet.

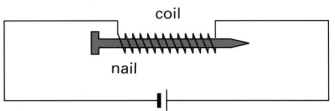

coil

nail

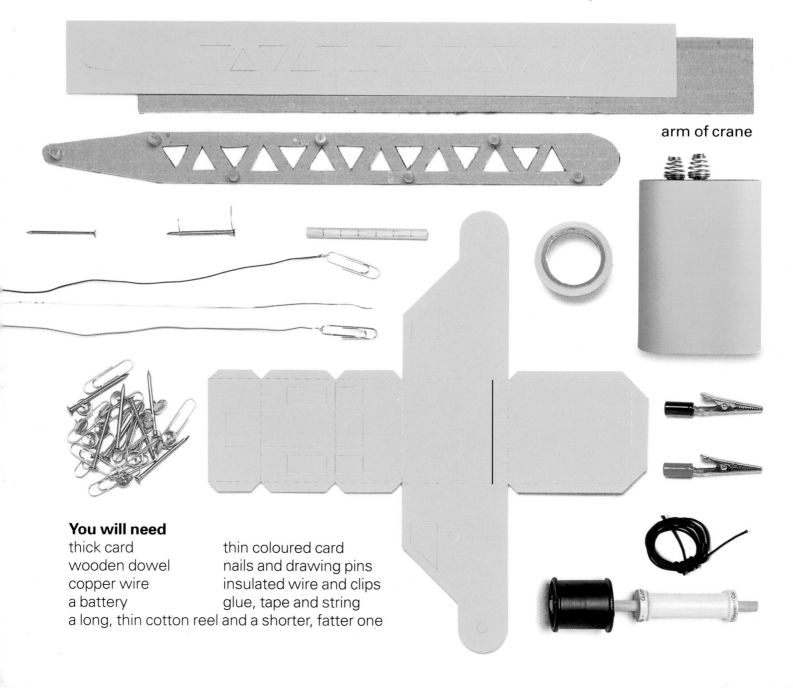

arm of crane

You will need

thick card	thin coloured card
wooden dowel	nails and drawing pins
copper wire	insulated wire and clips
a battery	glue, tape and string
a long, thin cotton reel and a shorter, fatter one	

1 Draw the shapes shown below onto the thick and thin card. Make sure that the line marked 'x' is the same length as the long, thin cotton reel.

2 Cut along the solid lines and fold along the dotted ones to assemble the body of the crane. Glue the thick card inside the body structure to make it stronger.

3 Put together the arm control winch as shown below, using the two cotton reels, dowels and a length of string.

4 Wrap copper wire around an iron nail to make an electromagnet. Then connect it to the battery with insulated wire, run over the top of the crane arm.

5 Tape the battery to the back of the crane. Check the circuit diagram to make sure the crane is correctly wired. When the leads and battery are connected the nail will become magnetized, and you can pick up a load of drawing pins. Disconnect and the pins will fall to the ground.

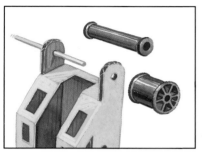

reinforcing card

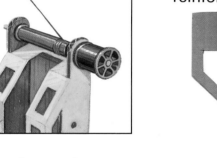

reinforcing card

base support

body of crane

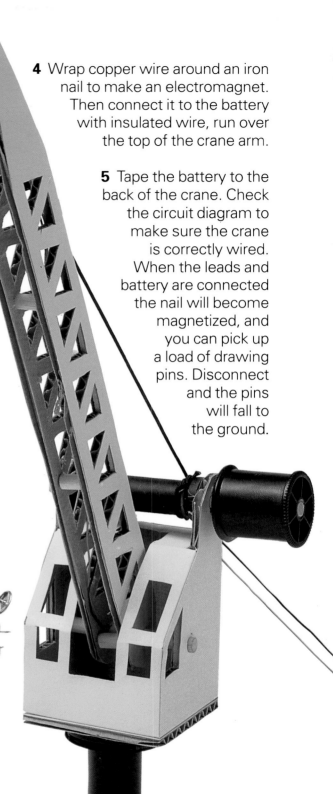

Electrical energy can be converted into mechanical energy, that is, energy that can pull and push and make things go. When electricity flows through the wires inside the motor, it makes them magnetic. The coil of wires becomes an electromagnet. It is attracted to fixed magnets inside the motor, which sets it off spinning around and around.

MAKE it WORK!

In this electric motor, a copper coil (the electromagnet) is connected to a battery by a clever little device called a **commutator**. The commutator brushes up against the wire leads of the electromagnetic coil, so that the electric current passes through; but the connections are loose enough to allow the coil to rotate freely.

As the coil turns, the connections of the commutator switch from side to side, so the direction of the electric current keeps changing. As the direction of the current changes, the poles of the electromagnet change sides too. The electromagnet is always attracted to the furthest fixed magnet and so it keeps on spinning and spinning.

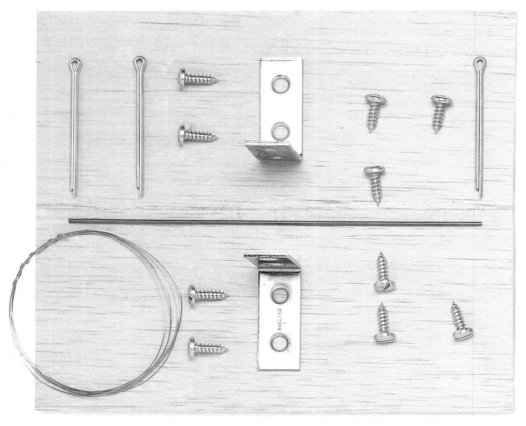

coil (electromagnet)

You will need

wood for the base	screws	copper wire	two strong magnets
two angle brackets	split-pin clips	balsa-wood block	insulating tape
thin copper tube	a metal spindle	crocodile clips/paper clips	a battery

1 Cut the base board out of a piece of balsa wood, or find a piece of soft wood. You could paint it a bright colour.

2 Ask an adult to drill a hole through the length of a small block of balsa wood. The hole should be wide enough in diameter for the copper tube to fit through.

4 Screw the angle brackets to the base board. Stick on the magnets and position them so that they attract one another. Ask an adult to drill three holes along the centre of the board for the split pins to stand up in.

5 Thread the metal spindle through the split pins and the balsa-wood block so that the coil is suspended and can turn easily.

6 Now make the commutator. You have to get the wires from the battery to touch the ends of the wire from the electromagnetic coil without stopping the coil spinning round and round. You should strip some of the casing from the ends of the wires and bend them inwards. Follow the illustration on the left.

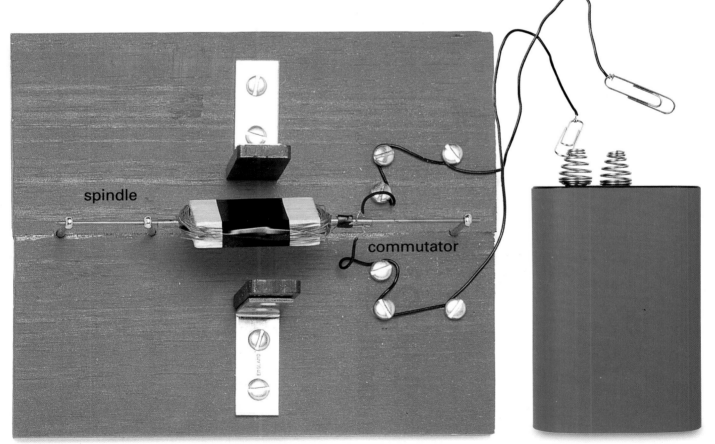

spindle

commutator

3 Cut grooves along two edges of the balsa-wood block and wrap copper wire tightly round the block. Insulate one end of the copper tube with clear sticky tape and fix the two ends of the coil wire in place with insulating tape as shown.

7 Screw the electrical wires into position so that the commutator connection is firmly fixed in place and cannot move. You may have to experiment a bit to get the screws positioned in the right place.

A simple electric motor turns a spindle round and round. One of the most direct and efficient ways of using this energy is to fix a propeller to the spindle. Boats are often driven by propellers in this way.

MAKE it WORK!

This propeller-driven boat makes good use of energy. It is designed with a propeller that drives through air rather than water because air is thinner than water and easier to move.

1 Make a balsa-wood framework for the hull and deck as shown on the right. Ask an adult to drill holes for the dowelling struts and glue them in place with a waterproof glue. Screw the electric motor in position. Paint the hull and deck with gloss paint.

2 Glue the battery onto the upper deck and wire up the circuit for the motor.

You will need

balsa wood
an electric motor
screws and nails
thin card

thin dowels
wire and clips
tape and glue
a propeller

To make the buoys

You can follow the instructions on page 31 to make marker buoys for your propeller boat.

3 Make the framework for the rudder by asking and adult to bend the metal wire as shown at right. Drill shallow holes in the wood for the metal wire to sit in. Now cut a rectangle of poster board for the rudder and tape it into place on the metal wire as shown.

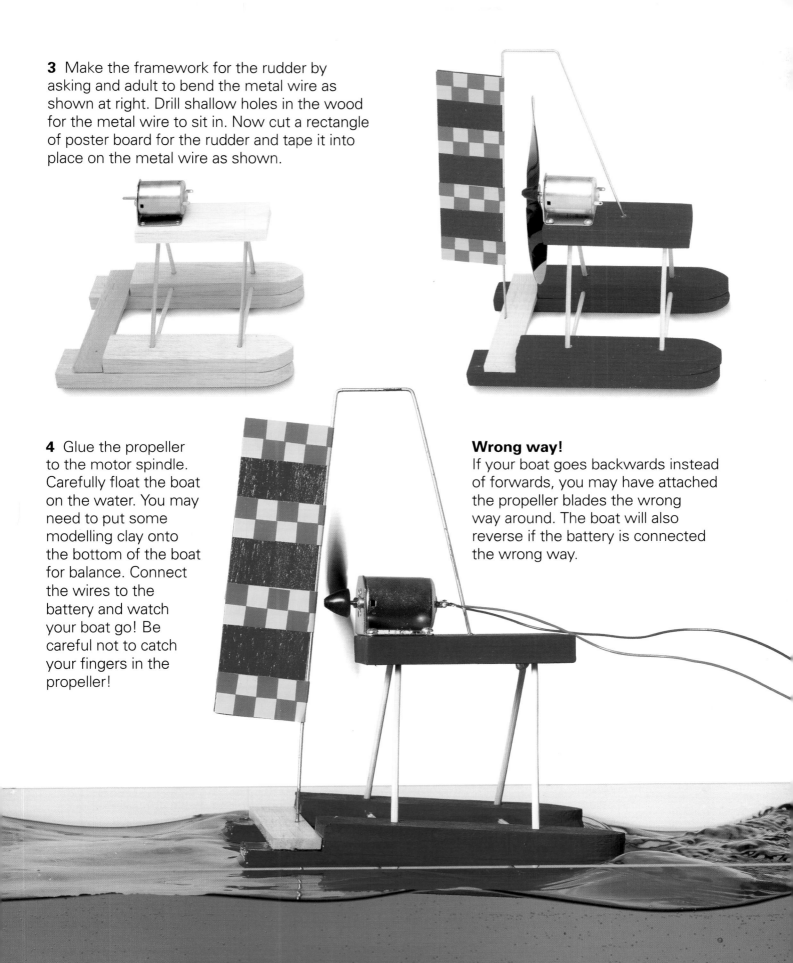

4 Glue the propeller to the motor spindle. Carefully float the boat on the water. You may need to put some modelling clay onto the bottom of the boat for balance. Connect the wires to the battery and watch your boat go! Be careful not to catch your fingers in the propeller!

Wrong way!
If your boat goes backwards instead of forwards, you may have attached the propeller blades the wrong way around. The boat will also reverse if the battery is connected the wrong way.

Modern high-speed electric trains are run by large electric motors. They take their power supply from overhead wires or electrified tracks. Not having to carry fuel increases their efficiency.

You will need

thin card	balsa wood
wooden dowelling	beads
an electric motor	paper clips
a battery	slices of cork
copper wire	upholstery pins
screws, thin nails and glue	
seven plastic bottle tops	
three thin copper strips	

1 Ask an adult to help you cut out the balsa-wood base of the engine. Then glue and nail the two roof supports into position as shown. Stick the upholstery pins into the supports.

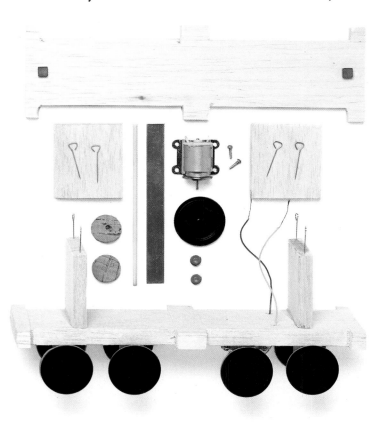

MAKE it WORK!

This model electric train works just like the real thing. The motor is on board but the power

is supplied through power lines overhead and is passed down to the motor through the upholstery pins.

2 Glue a plastic bottle top to the spindle of the electric motor to make a wheel. Screw the motor to the base of the train, and then pass two wires from the motor up through the base to the upholstery pins.

3 Ask an adult to drill two holes into each copper strip and bend them as shown to make the axle holders. Drill two more holes and screw the axle holders into the base.

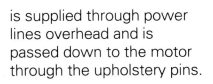

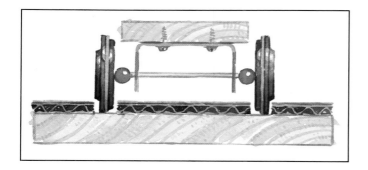

4 Make the axles by feeding the dowels through the axle holders. Then glue the beads and bottle tops to the ends of the axles to make the wheels.

6 Lay down three long strips of card to make two grooves for your train to run along. Add balsa-wood pylons overhead and fix a length of wire between them, threading it through the upholstery pins. Connect the overhead wires to the battery and watch your train go!

Extra carriages

Experiment making different kinds of carriages for your train. They do not need motors or wires, but you can make wheels and bases in the same way as for the engine. Join them up with small door magnets behind cork buffers.

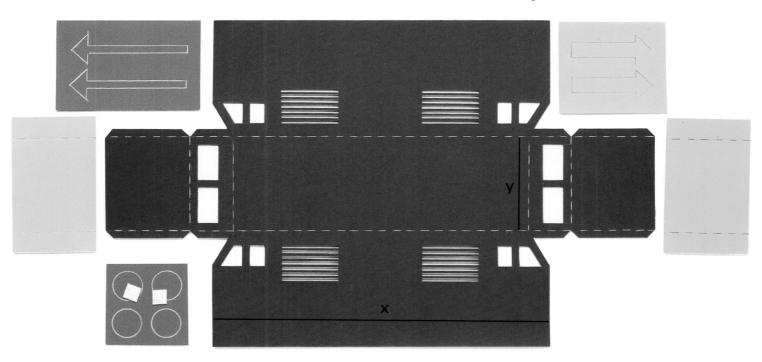

5 Mark out coloured card as shown, making sure that line 'x' is as long as the balsa-wood base and line 'y' is the same width. Assemble the body of the train and fit it over the base.

Running backwards and forwards

To make your train run the opposite way, just reverse the connections on the battery.

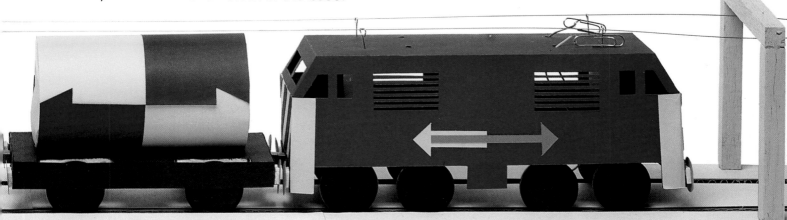

Electric motors range from the very small to the enormous. There are small battery–operated motors in model trains and clocks, but some electric motors in factories need a power supply so strong that it has to come directly from the power station.

MAKE it WORK!

See for yourself what happens if you change the supply to an electric motor. Build a spin-o-matico to make colourful patterns with paint. Compare the different results you get with different batteries.

1 Glue the two containers together, bottom to bottom, so you have two open ends. The top one will hold the paint, and the bottom one will hold the motor and wires.

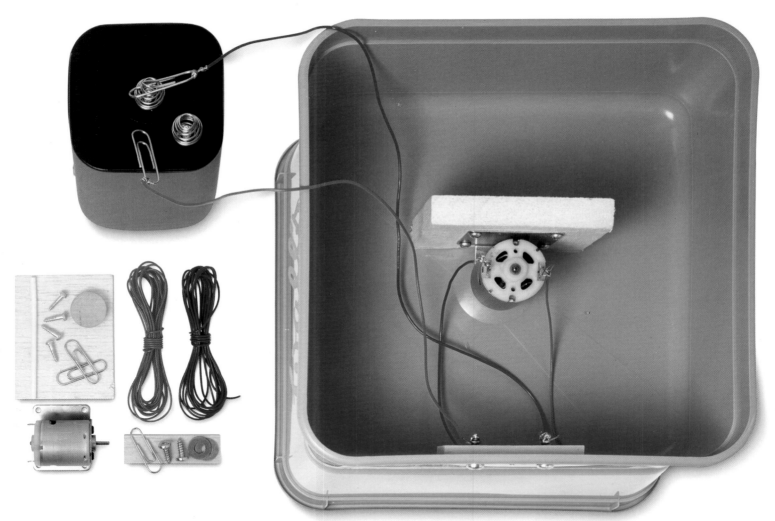

You will need

2 plastic containers	electric motor
2 different-sized batteries	paper clips
screws and washers	wire
slice of cork	wood
poster paint	glossy cardboard
glue and rubber cement	crocodile clips

2 Poke the spindle of the electric motor through the centre of the bottom container (the motor one), so it sticks up through the bottom of the top one (the paint holder). Screw the electric motor to a small piece of wood to hold it in place, and glue the wood to the container.

3 Make an on/off switch like the one shown on page 66, using a paper clip and two screws. Screw the paper clip to the outside of the container and onto a small piece of wood inside the container for support.

4 Wire the more powerful battery up to the motor, including the on/off switch in the circuit. To connect the wires to the switch, twist the ends of the wires around the screws, or attach them with crocodile clips.

5 Turn the containers over. Put a slice of cork over the top of the electric spindle that is poking up through the container. Test the motor to see if the cork spins when you switch it on.

6 Take a piece of cardboard and stick it onto the cork using a dab of rubber cement.

7 Switch the motor on and dribble paint onto the whirling card to make a pattern. You can also use a paint brush if you want to.

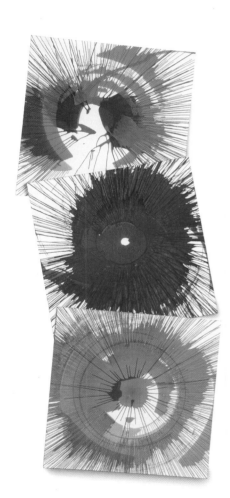

▲ Try doing some paintings using less power. Replace the powerful battery with the weaker one. How does the reduced power affect your finished painting?

When something is spinning very fast, the outside spins much faster than the inside. The force that seems to push everything towards the outside is called centrifugal force.

Sound

Did you know that sounds can blow out candles and crack glass? Or that bats use sounds to 'see' and find their way around? Have you ever wondered how different musical instruments produce completely different sounds?

MAKE it WORK!

Start experimenting with sound. Find out how sound waves are made, how they travel, and some of the surprising things they can do.

You will need

Most of the activities in this book use simple equipment, such as cardboard, glue and odds and ends. However, you will find some specialist equipment useful.

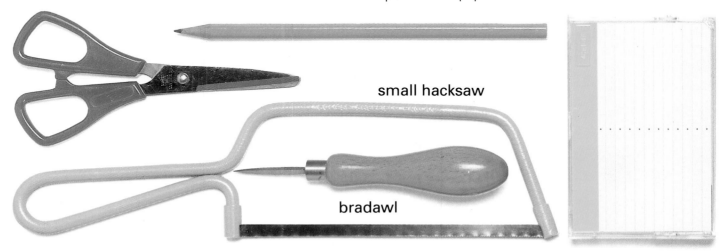

small hacksaw

bradawl

Investigating sound is part of the science of **physics**. Sound is a kind of energy, and it flows through the air in invisible waves. Everything that makes the air move, from the rustling of a leaf to the pounding of a big bass drum, sets off these **sound waves**, and creates a different kind of sound.

Small hacksaw and bradawl Some of the activities include making simple wooden supports or structures. You should always ask an adult to help if you are using saws, craft knives or other sharp tools.

Cardboard tubes These are handy for making musical instruments. You can use the insides of aluminium foil rolls or cardboard tubes made for carrying posters.

Music manuscript paper This is useful for writing down musical notes.

Copper wire This will be needed for making a simple radio and a telephone. Sound waves can be turned into an electrical pulse and then transferred along the wire. You can buy copper wire at any model shop or electrical supplier.

Balloons and rubber bands Some of the projects involve making a drum. Rubber from a balloon makes an excellent drumskin, and elastic bands will hold the rubber in place without tearing it.

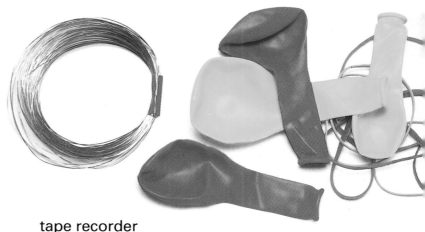

tape recorder

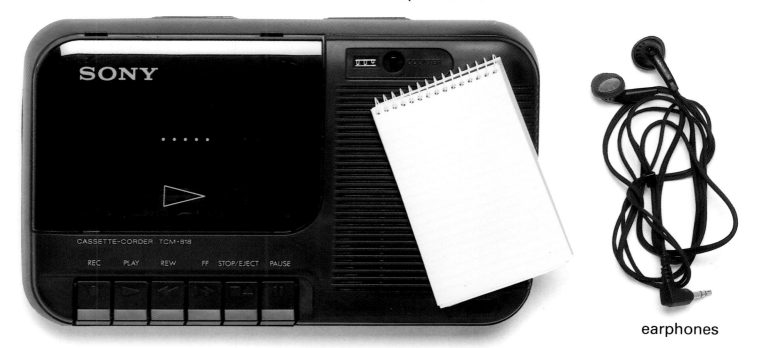

earphones

Tape recorder A simple tape recorder is the most useful piece of equipment for sound experiments. Ideally, you will need a small tape recorder or Walkman, along with a microphone, small headphones and some blank cassettes.

Plastic tubing and corks These can be bought from shops that sell do-it-yourself wine-making equipment.

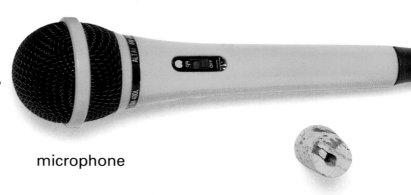

microphone

When we hear a noise, the sound waves usually travel to our ears through air, but sound can move through other substances too. Whales, for instance, hear a wide range of sound waves that move through water.

The sounds we hear are caused when a moving object makes the air **vibrate**. These vibrations travel through the air in the form of waves, and are picked up by our ears as sounds. The shape of the sound wave depends on the **pitch** of the sound. Low-pitched sounds are deep and rumbling, like a big bass drum. High-pitched sounds are shrill and piercing, like a tin whistle.

MAKE it WORK!

If you could see air, it would look like a great floating soup of gas particles. Low noises would make ripples a long way apart, and high-pitched sounds would make waves very close together. In fact, sound waves in air are invisible, but you can certainly prove they exist. Here are two ways to observe their effects.

For the sugar drum you will need

a cake tin	sugar
a wooden spoon	a balloon
large rubber bands	a baking tray

1 Cut out a circle of balloon rubber. Stretch it over the cake tin and fix it on with rubber bands.

2 Sprinkle a little sugar on the top of the drum.

3 Hold the baking tray above the drum and hit it with the wooden spoon. As the sound waves reach your ear, you hear the sound of the spoon on the tray. When those same waves hit the drumskin, they make it vibrate and you can see the sugar dancing up and down.

◀ Try holding the baking tray closer to the drum and then further away from it. Do you affect how much the sugar moves?

For the sound cannon you will need

a cardboard tube	candles
a piece of plywood	long nails
a plastic bag or a balloon	rubber bands

1 Ask an adult to help you hammer three nails through a piece of wood. Turn the wood over and push a candle onto each nail.

2 Take a length of cardboard tube. The inside of a roll of aluminium foil will do fine.

3 Stretch a circle of balloon rubber or plastic bag over each end of the tube and secure them with rubber bands.

4 Make a little hole in the plastic stretched over one end of the tube.

5 Ask an adult to light the candles.

6 Point the end of your sound cannon with the hole in it at one of the candles. Hold it just a short distance away.

7 Tap the other end with your finger. The vibrations you set up by tapping the drumskin travel to your ear as sound waves. The same vibrations move down the tube and push the air through the little hole at the opposite end, blowing out the candles.

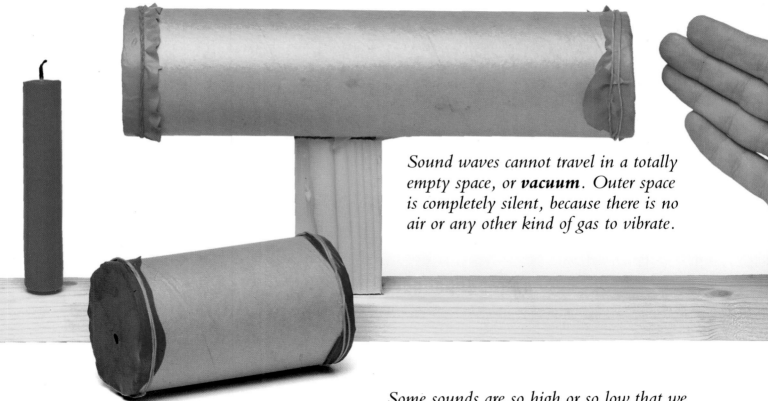

*Sound waves cannot travel in a totally empty space, or **vacuum**. Outer space is completely silent, because there is no air or any other kind of gas to vibrate.*

*Scientists measure sound waves by the number of times they make the air vibrate each second. One vibration, or cycle, per second is called one **Hertz** (Hz). When you hear a 700 Hz noise, the sound waves are hitting your eardrum 700 times per second. Scientists also measure other types of wave, such as light waves or radio waves, in Hertz.*

Some sounds are so high or so low that we cannot hear them. We are unable to make out sounds that have a frequency above roughly 20,000 Hz, or below 20 Hz. However, many animals have a much wider hearing range than humans. Bats and dogs, for instance, both pick up much higher sounds than we do. There are even special dog whistles that give out a high-pitched noise which only dogs can hear.

Our ears are specially designed to pick up vibrations in the air and turn them into **nerve pulses** which our brains understand as sounds. The working parts of our ears are actually inside our skulls. The whorled flaps that stick out on either side of the head are just funnels to collect sounds and pass them along to the **ear-drum**.

MAKE it WORK!

Make your own working model of a human ear. The ear-drum vibrates, moving three small bones inside the middle ear. These bones then move a fluid in a curly pipe called the **cochlea**. The cochlea is lined with minute hairs, and as the fluid moves, so do the hairs, sending tiny sound impulses along the nerves to the brain.

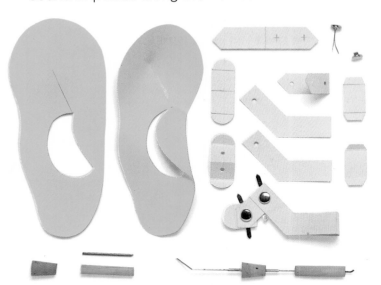

You will need

wood and nails	corks
thin dowels	thin card
hairy string	stiff wire
plastic tubing	a balloon
paper fasteners	tape and glue
a cardboard tube	food colouring

1 Take a length of cardboard tube and cut away part of one side as shown. Place a circle of balloon rubber over one end, fixing it securely with rubber bands. This will be the ear-drum.

2 Make the bones that are connected to the ear-drum – the **malleus**, the **incus** and the **stapes**. In the model, these bones are made from pieces of card. Cut out and fold the shapes shown in the photograph. Then glue and fix them together with paper fasteners as shown in the diagram on the right.

3 Stick the flaps of the cardboard malleus onto the rubber of the ear-drum with rubber solution glue.

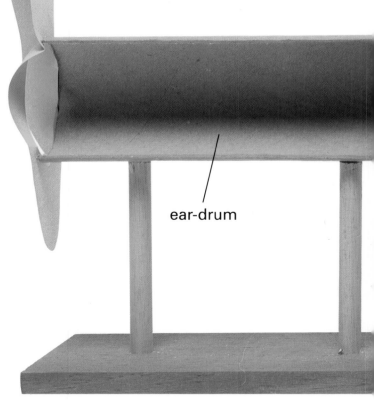

ear-drum

4 Cut a length of bendy, transparent plastic tubing and thread a slightly shorter length of string through it. Use a rough kind of twine, made out of natural fibres. The plastic tube is the cochlea, and the fibres on the twine are the tiny hairs that send nerve pulses to the brain.

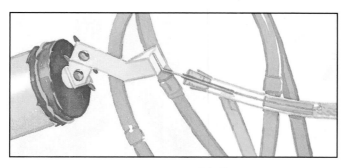

Making the middle ear

6 Ask an adult to drill a narrow hole in one cork stopper and push a small piece of thin copper tubing through the hole. Then thread the stiff wire through the copper tubing and stick it into the thinner piece of cork as shown.

7 Push the cork and wire mechanism into one end of the plastic tube. Almost fill the tube with water, and use the remaining cork to stop up the other end.

5 Connect the bones to the cochlea. Whittle down a piece of cork until it fits exactly inside the plastic tube. Cut two other corks so that they will stop up the ends of the tube.

8 Make a wooden base and put the separate parts of the model together, holding them up on dowelling supports. Glue the wire to the cardboard stapes and twist the cochlea into a spiral shape.

9 Make an ear shape from coloured card, and glue it to the free end of the tube.

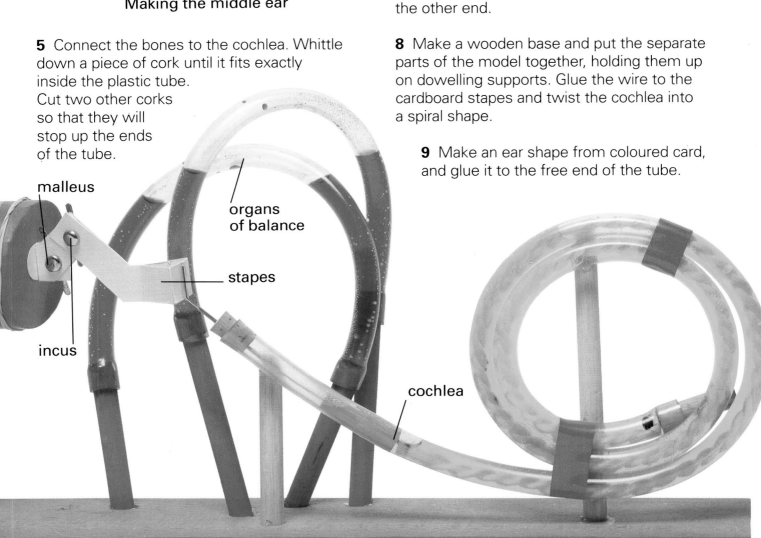

malleus

organs of balance

stapes

incus

cochlea

▲ Ears are important for other things besides hearing. They also help us to keep our balance. You can make your model ear even more authentic by adding semicircular tubes filled with coloured water. These represent the fluid canals that are our organs of balance.

Operating the model
To watch your model work, tap lightly on the inside of the ear-drum, to make it vibrate as though it had been hit by a sound wave. Can you see what happens to the little hairs on the string inside the cochlea tube?

Have you ever wondered why you have two ears, placed on either side of your head? It's so that you can tell which direction a sound is coming from. Unless a sound is directly in front of you, one ear will always pick it up slightly before the other. Your brain uses the different information coming from each ear to work out the direction of the sound.

MAKE it WORK!

To find out where a sound is coming from, we usually turn our heads until both ears hear the sound equally and the sound is 'in focus'. Make this game and test whether your ears have a good sense of direction.

You will need

large sheets of
   coloured paper or thin card
a pencil, scissors and string
some friends
a blindfold

*Noises behind us
sound muffled because
our ears are curved
forward to receive
sounds from in front.*

1 Take a large sheet of paper and fold it in half. Attach a pencil to one end of a length of string and fasten the other end of the string to the piece of paper at a corner along the fold.

2 Use the string and pencil like a compass to draw an arc. Then cut along the line, and unfold the paper to give you a semicircle. Repeat with another piece of paper the same size.

3 Put the two semicircles together to make a whole circle. If you wish, you can divide the semicircles into segments and make alternate colours. Then cut out a paper arrow.

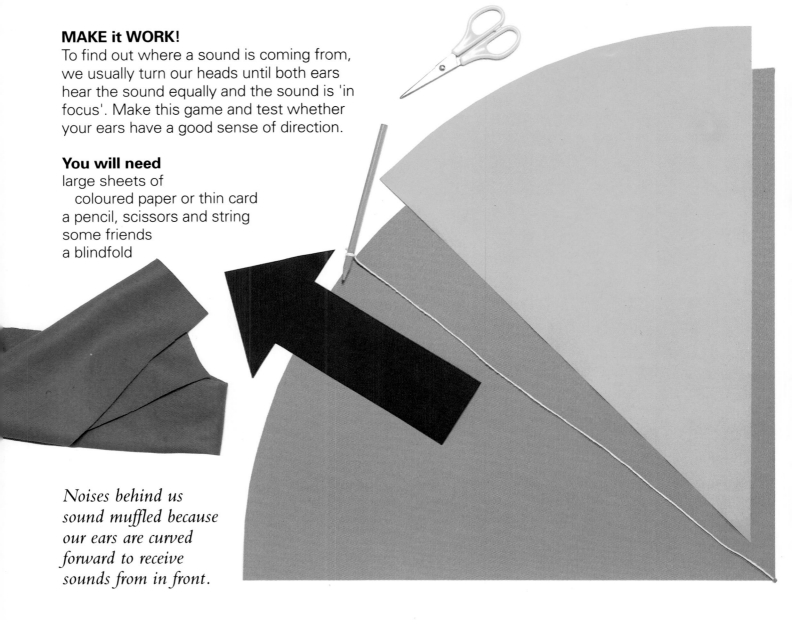

Compared with light, sound waves travel quite slowly — light moves almost a million times faster than sound. That's why, during a thunder storm, we see a flash of lightning before we hear a clap of thunder, even though they are both, in fact, caused at exactly the same time.

▼ Playing the game

This is a game for three to five people. One person volunteers to wear a blindfold and sits at the centre of the circle. The other players stand or sit silently around the circle, and someone makes a gentle noise, such as clicking their fingers. The blindfolded person points the arrow in the direction they think the sound is coming from. Each player can have a go at being blindfolded. Whose ears have the best sense of direction?

▶ Ask a friend to stand at the other side of a field or playground, holding up a handkerchief. (The further away your friend, the better the experiment will work — a pair of binoculars could help here.) Tell the friend to shout and drop the handkerchief at exactly the same time. You should see the handkerchief begin to fall before you hear the shout.

Instead of card, you could make the circle out of felt or other material.

Children have a wider range of hearing than adults. They can hear higher-pitched sounds.

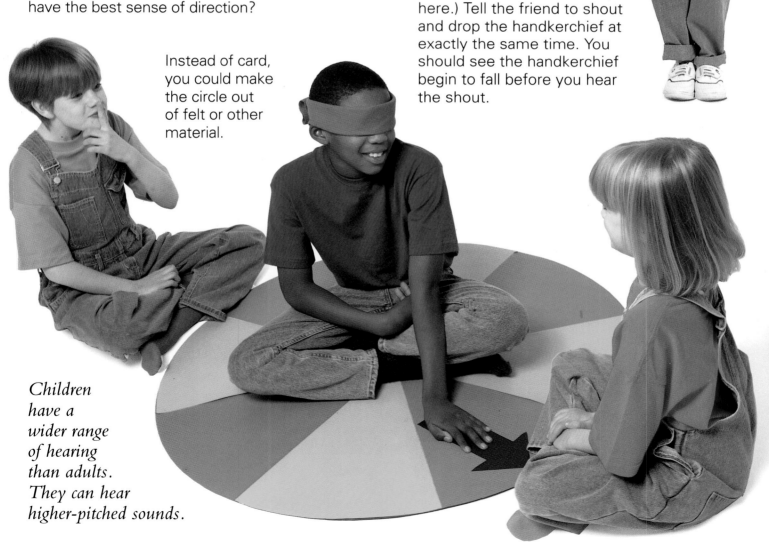

Our ears pick up the sound waves travelling through air, but, in fact, sound waves can travel through all kinds of substances. Whales, for instance, hear sound waves in water. And sound can even pass through a solid object, such as wood, if it is made to vibrate. However, sound doesn't pass very well from one type of substance to another. So if you shout at a brick wall, not much of the sound gets from the air through the wall and out at the other side. Instead, the sound waves bounce back off the wall again.

Angles of bounce

Sound waves in air will bounce off a flat, solid object at the same angle as they hit it – just like a ball bouncing off a wall. If, instead of a flat, solid object, the sound waves are bounced onto a surface that is soft or bumpy, the waves will break up and fade away.

You will need

thick card
a craft knife
cardboard tubes
a tape recorder and microphone
a clock or watch with a very soft tick

plasticine
an egg tray

MAKE it WORK!

In this experiment, you can control the path of the sound waves by directing them along cardboard tubes. The tubes hold the sound together, making it louder because the sound waves can't spread out and get lost in the air around them.

1 Take four equal lengths of cardboard tube, and cut three squares out of a piece of thick, smooth (not corrugated) card.

2 Use plasticine to fix the cardboard tubes and the squares of card in position as shown below. Each tube must be placed at exactly the same angle to the cards.

3 Measure the distance in a straight line between one end of the zig-zag and the other.

4 Set up your clock or watch away from the tubes, and record it ticking across the distance you have measured. Your microphone will pick up only a faint sound, or no sound at all.

5 Now position the clock at one end of the zig-zag, and record the sound that comes out of the other end.

6 If all of your tubes are positioned at the same angle, you should be able to record the ticking sound clearly. The sound waves travel down one tube, bounce on and off the reflector card at the end, and carry on back down the next tube.

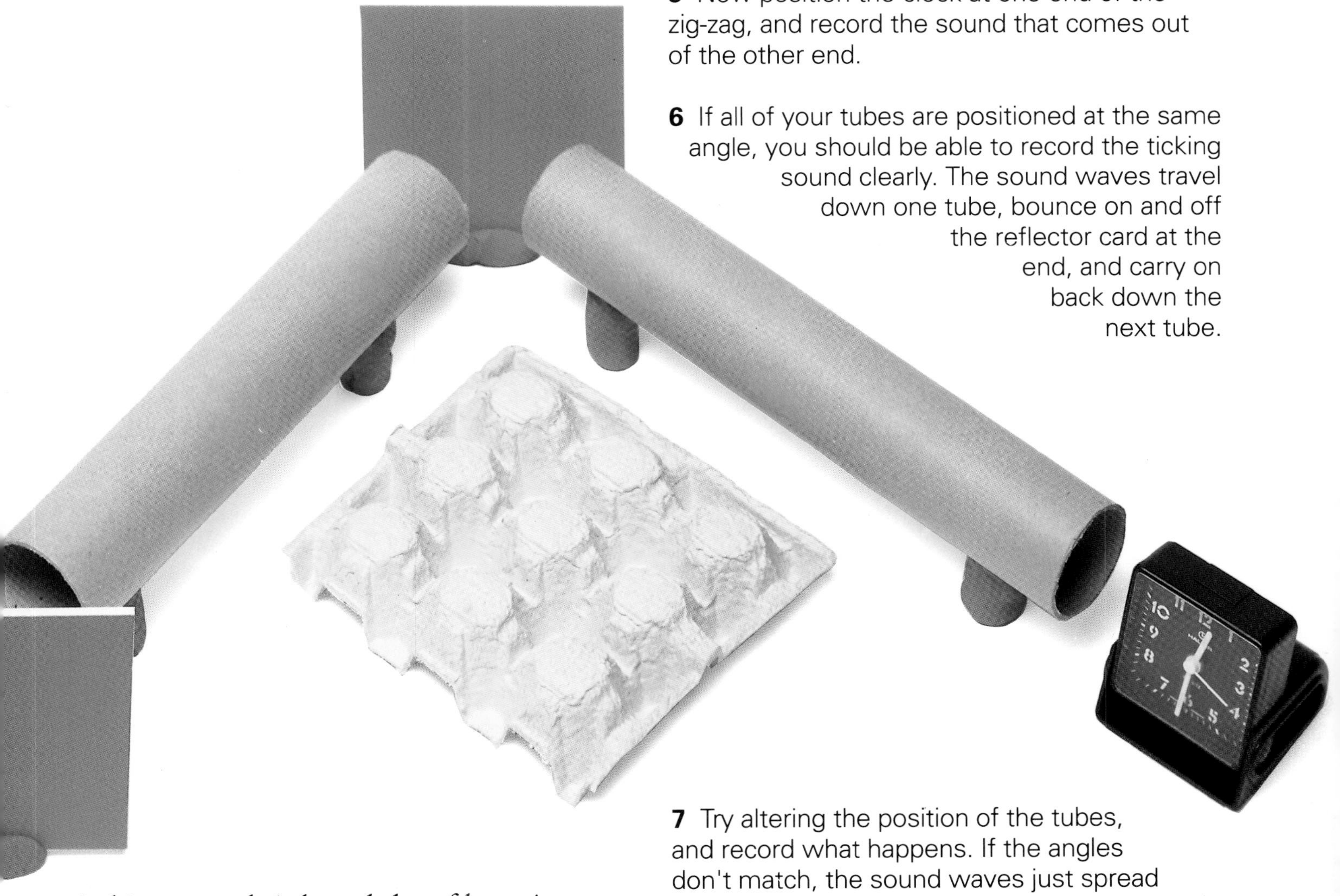

Architects use their knowledge of bouncing sound waves when they design new buildings. A noisy restaurant can be made much quieter by covering the floor, walls and ceiling with soft fabrics and bumpy surfaces to deaden the sound. But the stage and walls of a concert hall can be built to reflect sound waves, so that the music travels clearly towards where the audience is sitting.

7 Try altering the position of the tubes, and record what happens. If the angles don't match, the sound waves just spread out into the surrounding air, getting weaker and weaker.

Deadening sound

Put the cardboard tubes back in their original positions and then experiment with reflector cards made out of different materials. Cut some squares out of an old egg carton, so you can test the effect that a bumpy, uneven surface has on sound waves.

Before electronic hearing aids were invented, people who had difficulty hearing used an ear trumpet. They put the narrow end to their ear, and if someone spoke clearly into the wide end, their voice could be heard more clearly. The trumpet **amplified** the sounds, or made them louder.

The simplest amplifier is a big cone. It can be used to send out sounds or to listen to them. When it is used to send sounds, the cone holds the sound waves together, so they don't spread out in the air so quickly. When a cone is used to listen, like the old-fashioned ear trumpet, it collects sound waves from the air and directs them into the ear so they sound louder.

You will need

thin coloured card
flexible plastic tubing
two plastic funnels
glue
scissors

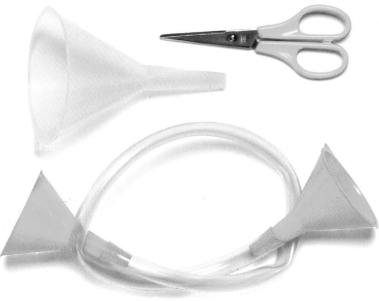

MAKE it WORK!

You can make some instruments to amplify sound waves. Doctors use a special listening device called a **stethoscope** to hear inside their patients' bodies. Normally, we can't hear the quiet gurgles and thumps made by our bodies, but the stethoscope picks up the sound waves and leads them directly into the doctor's ear.

Making a stethoscope

Take a length of plastic tubing that fits neatly over the narrow ends of the two funnels. Attach a funnel to each end.

Ask a friend to hold one funnel over his or her chest, put the other funnel to your ear and listen carefully. You will be able to hear your friend's heartbeat.

*The loudness of a sound is measured by the force with which the sound wave pushes the air. The units of measurement are called **decibels** – named after the scientist and inventor Alexander Graham Bell.*

Making an ear trumpet and a loud-hailer

1 Take a sheet of thin coloured card and roll it into a cone shape. One end should be wide, to collect sound waves, and the other end should be narrow enough to fit into your ear.

2 Make the loud-hailer cone in the same way, but the narrow end should be slightly larger so that you can speak into it.

3 Once you have the right cone shapes, tape or glue the card. Trim the ends and decorate the cones with coloured paper shapes of bright, contrasting colours.

4 To test the loud-hailer, ask a friend to stand so far away that you can't hear each other's voices. Then speak normally through the cone.

5 To test the ear trumpet, point it towards a quiet noise. You will be able to hear the sound more clearly. **Be careful**! Never shout down an ear trumpet at anyone. You could damage their ear-drum.

On the decibel scale, 0 is absolute silence. A falling leaf would measure 20 decibels, a conversation about 50 and a clap of thunder 110. Above 140 decibels, sounds become painful and may damage the ear-drum.

Sound waves can be converted from sound energy into electrical energy and back again. That's how sounds can be carried over long distances by the telephone. The sound waves are turned into an electrical pulse, which travels down the telephone wire to the receiver – just like the nerve pulses that carry sounds from our ears to our brains.

MAKE it WORK!

Modern telephones use carbon granules to convert sound waves into electrical pulses. However, you can make a simple telephone for yourself, using magnets and copper wire.

When you speak into the yoghurt pot, the paper drumskin vibrates, so that the magnet bounces up and down inside a coil of copper wire. This movement causes an electrical charge, which passes down the wire. At the other end of the wire, another copper coil, magnet and drumskin convert the electrical pulses back into sound waves.

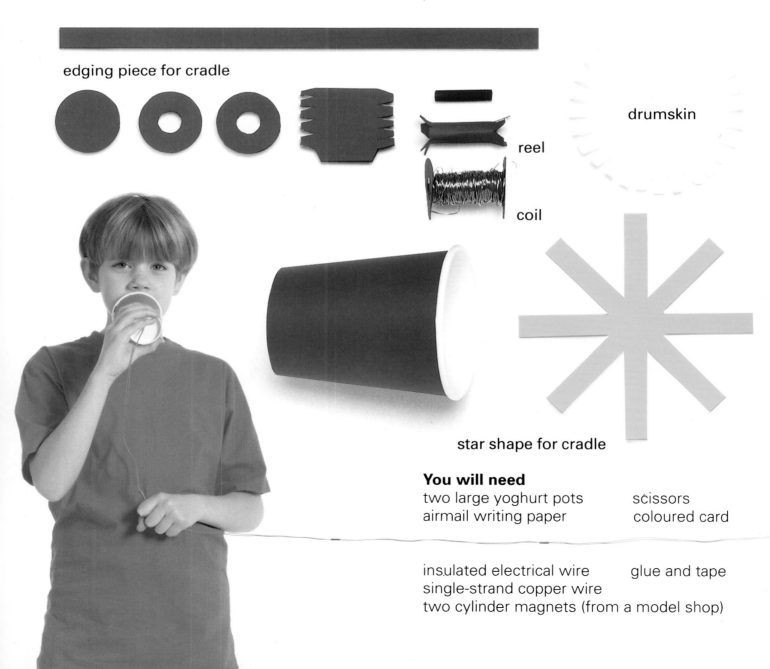

edging piece for cradle

drumskin

reel

coil

star shape for cradle

You will need

two large yoghurt pots
airmail writing paper

scissors
coloured card

insulated electrical wire
single-strand copper wire
two cylinder magnets (from a model shop)

glue and tape

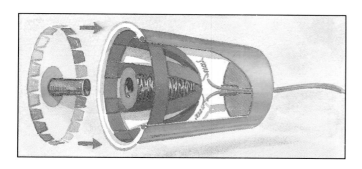

1 First make two copper coils. Cut and glue the pieces of card as shown to make reels that will fit neatly around the cylinder magnets. Wind a long piece of copper wire around each reel forty or fifty times.

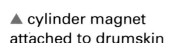

▲ **cylinder magnet attached to drumskin**

▲ **cradle**

2 Cut star shapes and edging pieces out of thick card as shown. Then put them together to make cradles for the reels and copper coils.

3 Pass two equal lengths of insulated wire through the bottom of each yoghurt pot and connect them to the ends of the copper coils.

▶ If your connecting wire is long enough, you can use this phone to speak to a friend in another room.

4 Cut a drumskin out of thin airmail paper. Snip the edges so that you can glue it to fit tautly inside the rim of each yoghurt pot.

5 Now assemble each yoghurt-pot receiver. First, glue the reel and coil into the cradle. Fix the cradles inside the yoghurt pots as shown.

6 Glue the magnet to a small circle of card and glue this card in turn onto the back of the paper drumskin. Then glue the drumskin in place. Check that the magnet fits neatly inside the reel, but has room to move freely up and down.

7 To talk into the telephone, cup your hands around the pot and talk right at the drumskin. To listen, hold the drumskin up to your ear.

Some modern telephone wires now use optical fibres, which transfer sound not as an electrical pulse, but as a high-speed beam of light.

Sound was first recorded by a machine called a **phonograph** – a kind of early record player. A needle was attached to a drumskin, stretched across the narrow end of a sound horn. When someone shouted into the horn, the needle would vibrate. As the needle bounced up and down, it recorded the sound waves as grooves on a cylinder coated in wax or tin foil.

Tape recordings

Sound recording techniques have come a long way since the days of the phonograph. Sound is now recorded onto magnetic tape. In the tape recorder, the sound waves are turned into electric impulses. These are stored on the tape as a sequence of different magnetic blips.

MAKE it WORK!

A microphone is a kind of electric ear. It turns sound waves into electric signals. However, it may have trouble picking up sounds not made close by. You can improve a simple microphone by putting it inside an umbrella! Its shape will collect the sound waves and reflect them back to the microphone.

To play a phonograph recording, the cylinder was rotated underneath the needle. The pattern of bumps and dips in the cylinder grooves vibrated the needle, which the drumskin and sound horn turned back into sound waves.

You will need

a tape recorder	tapes
a microphone	earphones
sticky tape	an umbrella
three or four friends who can sing	

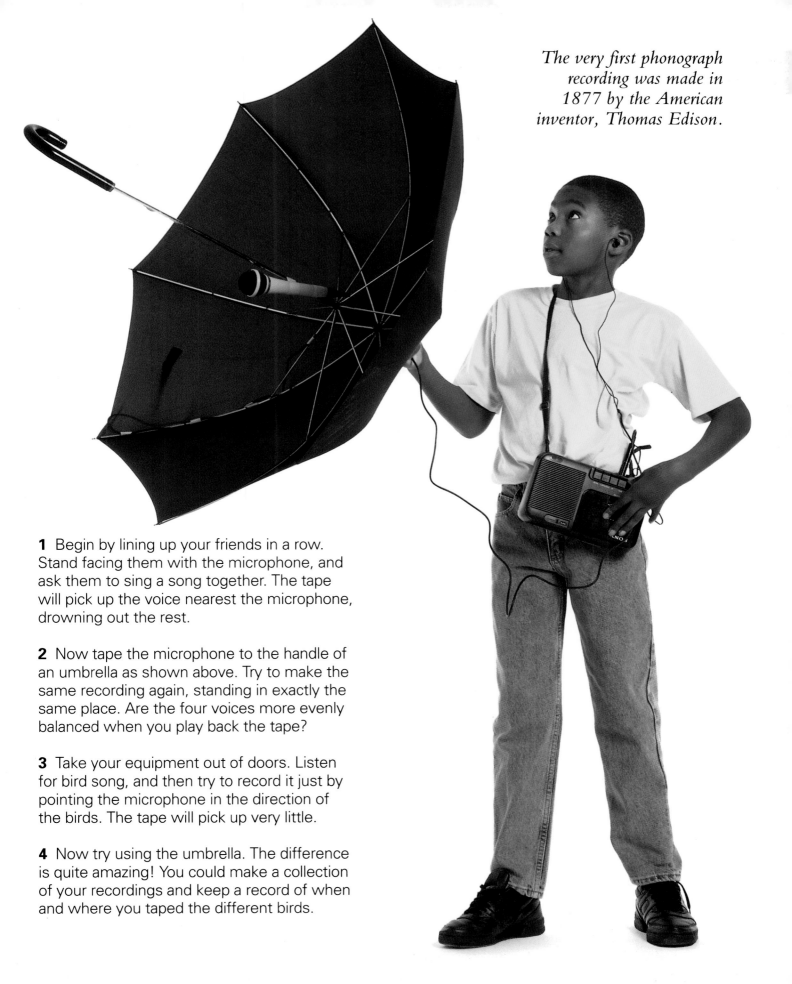

The very first phonograph recording was made in 1877 by the American inventor, Thomas Edison.

1 Begin by lining up your friends in a row. Stand facing them with the microphone, and ask them to sing a song together. The tape will pick up the voice nearest the microphone, drowning out the rest.

2 Now tape the microphone to the handle of an umbrella as shown above. Try to make the same recording again, standing in exactly the same place. Are the four voices more evenly balanced when you play back the tape?

3 Take your equipment out of doors. Listen for bird song, and then try to record it just by pointing the microphone in the direction of the birds. The tape will pick up very little.

4 Now try using the umbrella. The difference is quite amazing! You could make a collection of your recordings and keep a record of when and where you taped the different birds.

Bats have poor eyesight, but a very good sense of hearing. They can hear ultrasound – very high-pitched sounds, way beyond the human hearing range. Bats can use these sounds to find their way around the dark caves where they live. When a bat makes a high-pitched squeak, the sound bounces off the wall of the cave and returns to the bat as an ultrasound echo. From the amount of time between the squeak and echo, the bat can tell how far away the wall is.

1 Take a rectangle of black card, fold it over and draw the shape of a bat wing as shown above. Cut out this shape, unfold the card and you'll have a symmetrical bat. Make twelve bats, three for each player.

MAKE it WORK!

Make this ultrasound game, and turn over the page to find out how to play. The board is a dark cave, criss-crossed by sound waves. The playing pieces are bats, and they use the sound waves as flight paths to move from one wall of the cave to another.

You will need

corks and glue
wooden dowels
a cocktail stick
thick coloured card
thin coloured card
a craft knife or scissors
Velcro dots or paper clips

2 Take a piece of cork for each bat. Stick a Velcro dot underneath the cork, and then glue the cork itself to the side of the bat, with the ears facing up.

3 If you can't get hold of any Velcro dots or corks, simply attach a paper clip to the bottom of each bat as shown on the left. Velcro bats will sit on top of the sound waves. Paper-clip bats, on the other hand, hang beneath the sound waves.

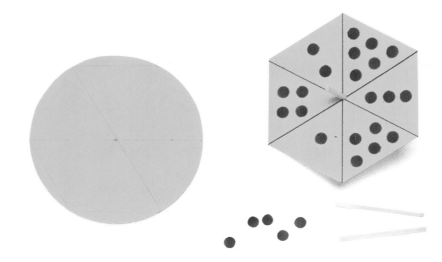

4 Choose a colour for each player. Put different coloured dots on each player's bats.

5 Make the spinner. Draw a circle and divide it into six segments. Snip off the sides to make a hexagon, and stick on the coloured dots.

6 Poke a cocktail stick through the middle of the spinner. Twirl it around and it will come to rest on one of the six sides.

 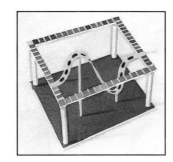

Assembling the board

7 Now make the board. Cut a large square of card for the base, and glue a length of dowel standing on its end in each corner.

8 Cut four strips of thick card, each as long as a side of the baseboard. Divide each strip into sixteen small squares. Glue these strips in place on the wooden dowels, to make the raised section of the board as shown in the diagram above.

9 At each corner of the raised section put a square of paper in one of the players' colours.

10 Cut six long strips of thin card to represent sound waves. If you have made Velcro bats, mark off the sound waves with Velcro spots. If you have paper-clip bats, stick a row of coloured-paper spots on each sound wave.

11 Put the sound waves in position, stretching the strips of thin card in wavy lines across the board from one raised side to the other. In some places, you will have to add extra dowel supports to hold up the sound waves and help them to keep their shape.

Playing the ultrasound game

In this game, each player has three bats which set off from the corner marked in their colour. The aim of the game is to make as many flights as possible from one side of the board to the other within a set time limit.

1 Decide on your time limit for the game – say fifteen or thirty minutes.

2 Spin the spinner. The player with the highest number starts, and play passes to the left.

3 Players spin in turn and move their bats along the edge of the playing board. When a bat reaches the beginning of a sound wave, it may cross the cave, spot by spot.

4 Each time a bat completes a crossing, the player puts a scoring counter or old button in his or her corner of the cave. The bat continues around the edge of the board until it reaches another sound wave.

5 Players may use a spin to move any one of their bats. They may also split the score and move more than one bat.

6 When two bats going in opposite directions meet, they cannot pass one another. The two players both spin the spinner. The bat with the higher score continues its flight, but the lower-scoring bat falls off and goes back to its corner.

7 At the end of the agreed time limit, the players have a race back to their corners, completing any waves they have already started. The first player to bring all three bats home gets three extra counters.

8 The winner is the player who has collected the most counters.

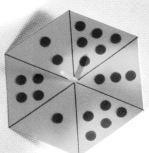

Radio transmitters send sounds around the world, by changing sounds into electrical impulses and then **radio waves**. These waves of energy travel at the speed of light through air, solid objects, and empty space. Radio receivers pick up the waves and turn them back into sounds again.

MAKE it WORK!

Make your own simple radio receiver and try tuning into radio signals. Remember that the signals will be weaker than a normal radio.

Warning: This crystal radio does not need a power supply and must NEVER be connected to an electrical outlet.

You will need

two rubber bands	thick balsa wood
an awl	16 in. steel wire
wood glue	a large metal paper clip
paint	a germanium diode,
a sharp craft knife	and a crystal earpiece
wire strippers	from a hobby shop

22 ft. bare (non-insulated, non-lacquered) copper wire
a cardboard tube, 9 in. long
three nuts, bolts, and washers
33 ft. single-strand insulated electrical wire

1 Ask an adult to help you to cut a 9 in. x 4 in. piece of balsa wood for the base. Cut out four balsa wood feet and glue them to the corners.

2 Make two supports for the tube, by cutting out semicircles from the balsa wood. Glue into position on the base. Paint the wood.

3 Use the awl to make three small holes along the front of the base at **a**, **b**, and **c**. Put a washer over each hole. Push the bolts into the base and fix them under the board with nuts.

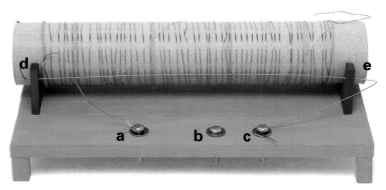

4 Take the bare copper wire and leaving one short end free at **e**, carefully wind the rest around the cardboard tube. The coils **must not** touch each other.

5 Secure the copper wire with rubber bands at both ends of the tube. Then wrap the long end of the copper wire around the bolt at **a**.

6 Push the steel wire through the balsa wood supports in front of the copper coil, from **d** to **e**. Leave a short end at **d**, pushing it upward to secure. Bend the long end at **e** forward and wrap it around the bolt at **c**.

▲ The **diode** detects radio waves picked up by the **antenna** so that you can hear sounds in the earpiece.

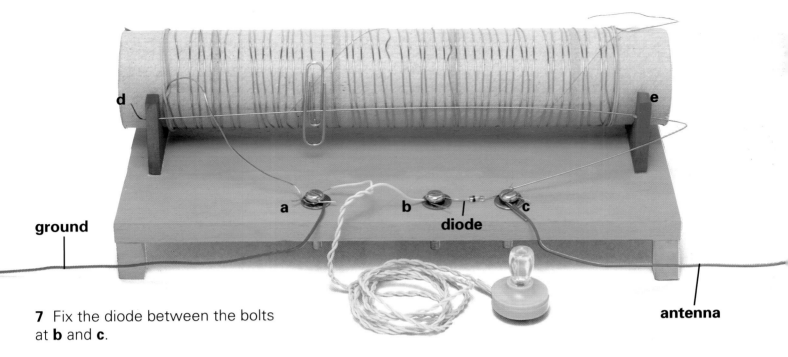

7 Fix the diode between the bolts at **b** and **c**.

8 Strip the insulation from the ends of both earpiece leads, using the wire strippers. Attach one end to the bolt at **a**, so that it touches the wire. Wrap the other end around the bolt at **b**.

9 To make an antenna, cut 30 ft. of insulated wire. Strip off the insulation at one end of the wire and tie it around the bolt at **c**. Tie the other end to a post or tree in an outside space.

10 To ground the radio, take 3 ft. of insulated wire and strip the covering from both ends. Attach one end to the bolt at **a**, and the other to a metal object, such as a clean, unpainted metal railing.

NOTE
1. Keep surfaces of all connections clean.
2. Make sure all connections touch in the correct places, and nowhere else.
3. If you use lacquered copper wire, you must sandpaper the ends where they wrap around the bolts, and where the paper clip touches the copper wire.
4. Weather and location may affect reception. Your receiver will probably work best in a large open space away from tall buildings.
5. Try using different objects as antennas, and to ground your radio.

▼ To operate the radio, put in the earpiece and slip a metal paper clip onto the steel wire between **d** and **e**. Twist it backward, and move it slowly along the copper coil. You should hear faint clicks or a radio station. What the radio picks up depends on the number of turns of copper wire.

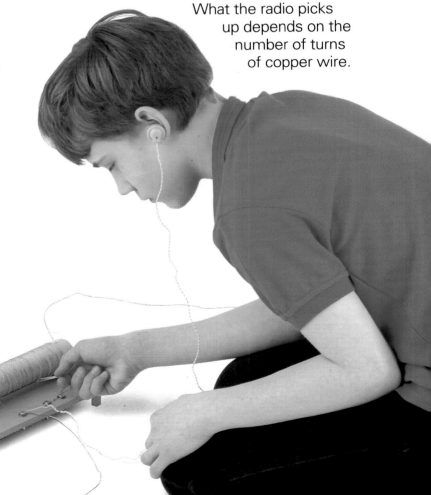

Every sound has its own pitch – high or low – depending on the shape of the sound wave. To a musician, each different pitch of sound makes an individual musical **note**.

Musical notes can be arranged in a special pattern called a **scale**. There are many kinds of scale, but the most common is called an **octave**. It is made up of eight notes that move higher and lower step by step. The notes on a piano are set out in octaves – and you might have sung the notes of an octave yourself: do, ray, me, fa, so, la, te, do.

MAKE it WORK!

Make your own instruments that play the notes of the octave scale. You will need to learn the notes of the octave, or copy them from a musical instrument – an instrument with fixed notes, such as a piano or electric organ, is easiest. If you don't play an instrument yourself, you could ask for some help from a friend or adult who does.

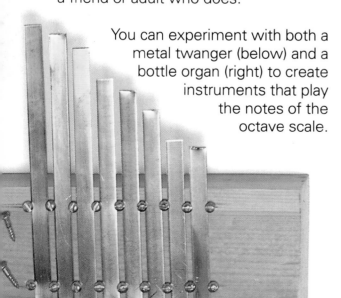

You can experiment with both a metal twanger (below) and a bottle organ (right) to create instruments that play the notes of the octave scale.

For the bottle organ you will need

food colouring   a long nail
a musical instrument
eight bottles of the same size and shape

1 Collect eight identical bottles and set them up in a line. (Milk bottles are probably the easiest to use.) Hit each bottle with a long nail. They should all make the same sound.

2 Take a jug of water and pour a little into the first bottle. If you are going to copy a scale from a musical instrument, play the first note of the scale. Then gently hit the top of the bottle with the nail to see if it sounds close to the note you have just played. Gradually adjust the water level in the bottle until both bottle and instrument give out exactly the same note.

3 Follow the same method for each bottle until you have made a complete octave.

4 When you are happy with the sound of the bottle organ, dye the water in each bottle with a few drops of food colouring. You will be able to see the different notes more easily.

5 Now try to pick out a tune – something simple, such as 'Three Blind Mice'.

Making a metal twanger

You can make another octave scale using strips of metal or thick steel wire, fixed to a solid block of wood beneath the heads of screws.

For a brass twanger you will need

a small block of wood	a file
a thin strip of brass	screws
a small hacksaw	a screwdriver
a bradawl	a hammer

Be careful! To make a twanger, you will have to use sharp tools. Ask an adult to help you.

1 Cut a short strip of brass and hold it in place on the block of wood. Pluck the end of the strip, and it will make a twanging noise.

2 Now cut seven other strips of brass, each slightly longer than the last. Experiment with different lengths until you can arrange the strips on the block of wood to make an octave.

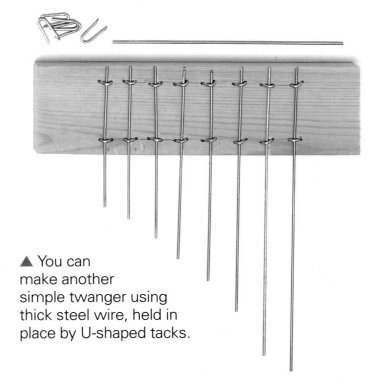

▲ You can make another simple twanger using thick steel wire, held in place by U-shaped tacks.

3 File the sharp edges off the strips of brass and fix them in place. Mark where the screws should go with a bradawl and then twist them into the wood with the screwdriver.

▼ Musicians check the pitch of an instrument with a tuning fork. When the fork is struck, its prongs vibrate at a regular speed, sending out a clear, single note that never changes.

A lot of the pop music and classical music we hear is based on the eight-note scale, but some styles use totally different scales. Much Chinese music is based on a sequence of five notes; Indian classical music often uses a twenty-two note scale.

How many kinds of musical instrument can you think of? They come in many different shapes and sizes, from mouth organ to double bass, synthesiser to tom-tom drums. Yet they all have one thing in common – they create sounds by making the air vibrate.

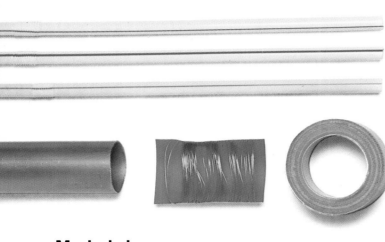

Musical pipes
Many musical instruments have pipes – organ pipes, the curly tube of a French horn or the thin, straight pipe of a tin whistle. Inside each pipe is a column of air. When this air is made to vibrate in a certain way, the pipe plays a note.

MAKE it WORK!
Make your own music using pipe instruments. Panpipes are a set of pipes of different lengths, each of which makes a different note. Tubular bells are metal pipes that hang free and make a bell-like sound when hit with a large nail.

To make the panpipes
1 Cut eight straws or eight pieces of plastic tubing to different lengths. Tape them together, stepped at one end, as shown above.

2 To play the panpipes, blow gently across the top of each pipe to produce a note. You will find that longer pipes make a lower note than shorter pipes.

You will need
glue
wood
copper pipe
nylon fishing line
bendy plastic tubing   sticky tape
screws and a screwdriver   a hacksaw
plastic drinking straws   a large nail

3 Experiment with the lengths of the pipes. Can you make octave scales like those on the previous page?

To make the tubular bells

1 Ask an adult to help you cut eight lengths of copper pipe. Each one should be a little longer than the one before, so that you can arrange them in a stepped pattern.

4 Hang the copper pipes from the top piece of the frame using lengths of strong fishing twine. Thread the twine through the holes you have drilled, and attach it to the copper pipes with strong plastic tape.

Pipes that give out a sound when they are struck are **percussion instruments**. *Pipes that are blown to make music are* **wind instruments**.

2 Make a wooden frame. It should be big enough to hold the copper pipes hanging at well-spaced intervals. You will need a flat base, two side pieces and a top piece.

3 Drill eight holes at equal spaces through the top piece of the frame. Then put the frame together, cutting the side supports into the baseboard. Glue the joints and secure them firmly with screws.

5 Arrange the pipes in order of length. Strike them with a metal nail to make them chime.

Because the pipes hang free, they carry on vibrating after they have been hit, and the sound lingers on. Try striking a note and then grasp hold of the pipe tightly with your hand. The sound dies straight away. As soon as you stop the pipe vibrating, the sound waves stop being produced too.

Unlike our panpipes, many instruments create sounds by vibrating the air in just a single pipe. In these instruments, the different notes are made by altering the length of the main pipe. Recorders have holes to let the air out in different places. A brass trombone has a slide that moves up and down to change its length.

1 Take a length of copper pipe or a section of cardboard tubing. Leave a space at one end, and then use a bradawl to mark out evenly-spaced holes along the rest of the pipe.

2 Ask an adult to drill the holes you have marked. At the end of the pipe nearest the mouthpiece, cut a blowhole, following the diagram on the right.

▼ **tin whistle**

▼ **brass-pipe recorder**

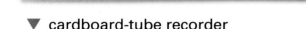

▼ **cardboard-tube recorder**

▲ ▼ **gazoos**

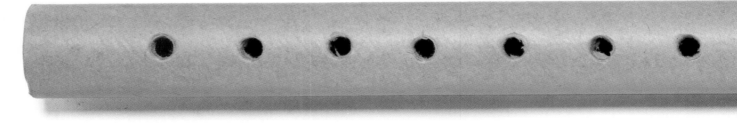

Make a recorder
A recorder player makes different notes by putting fingers over the holes to make the air travel further down the pipe.

To make a recorder you will need
wooden dowelling	a cork
a tube of thick cardboard	copper pipe
a bradawl, drill and hacksaw	

3 Cut a slice off a piece of cork to give it a flat edge. Then sandpaper the cork to make it smooth and fit snugly inside the top of the recorder pipe. Position the flat side face up, opposite the blowhole and finger holes.

4 Now blow gently into the mouthpiece. The cork and the blowhole are shaped so that the air inside the recorder is vibrated.

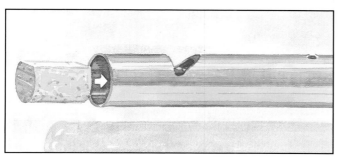

Making the recorder mouthpiece

To make a gazoo you will need
a copper pipe   sticky tape or glue
wooden dowelling
the mouthpiece from a party blower

1 Ask an adult to cut a length of pipe.

2 Cut a piece of dowelling about 15 cm (6 in) longer than the pipe. The dowelling should fit inside the pipe as tightly as possible, while still being able to move easily.

3 Fit the party blower mouthpiece to one end, using glue or sticky tape. If you cannot find a mouthpiece that fits, you can still play the gazoo by blowing across the top of the pipe.

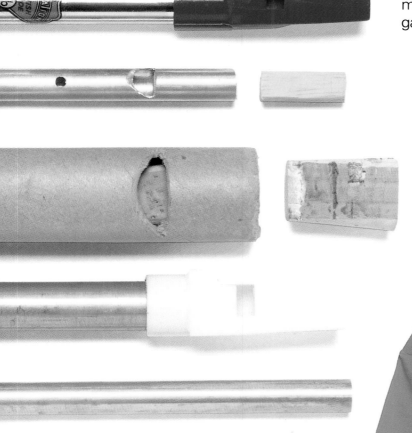

Make a gazoo
Gazoos make a weird wailing sound. The length of the pipe is changed by pushing a dowel in and out. There are no separate notes, just a continuous rising and falling tone.

The width of a pipe, as well as its length, will affect the sound it makes. Narrow pipes make higher-pitched notes than wide pipes.

Shakers and rattles are all percussion instruments. They are often used to stress the rhythm of a piece of music and give it a strong beat. Shakers, like our paper-cup shakers, make the air vibrate by moving loose objects inside an enclosed space. Rasps and rattles rub together two rough surfaces to set up sound vibrations.

MAKE it WORK!

Make your own collection of different shakers and rattles. They could make a whole variety of sounds, depending on the amount of air that is made to vibrate and the kinds of surface that are rubbed up against one another.

To make the shakers you will need

paper cups   sticky tape
plastic bottles with lids
rice, lentils, chickpeas, beads and pebbles

1 To make a paper-cup shaker, put a handful of rice or lentils into one cup. Turn another cup upside down and tape the two cups together, rim to rim.

2 To make plastic-bottle shakers, simply pour a handful of beads or chickpeas into the bottle, and put the lid on tight. You could decorate the shakers with coloured paper if you wish.

3 Try making shakers with different-sized bottles. You will find that larger bottles which hold more air make deeper sounds.

▲ Experiment with different fillings for your shakers. You will find that paper-cup shakers with lentils make a softer sound than plastic bottles with chickpeas.

To make a rattle you will need

a wooden dowel or stick   a hammer
several long, thin nails   enamel paints
metal bottle tops   a large, thick nail

1 Punch a hole in the middle of each bottle top using the hammer and large nail. **Be careful** as you do this! Make sure that you've put a piece of old wood underneath the bottle top, and concentrate so that you don't hit your fingers.

2 Slip four bottle tops onto each thin nail. (If you like, you could give them a coat of enamel paint first.) Then hammer the nails into the dowel or stick, making sure the tops can rattle freely.

To make a sandpaper rasp you will need

two blocks of wood   drawing pins
two sheets of sandpaper

1 Pin the sandpaper to the blocks of wood as shown below.

2 To play the rasp, rub the two sandpaper surfaces together. It makes a soft, grating noise.

To make a wooden rasp you will need

a block of soft wood   a large nail
a small hacksaw

1 Ask an adult to help you cut a zig-zag shape along the top of the block of wood as shown.

2 To play the wooden rasp, run the nail back and forth along the uneven surface. It makes a harsher sound than the sandpaper rasp.

Both of these rasps make quite soft noises. Unlike the shakers, they have no space inside them where the air can vibrate to make the sounds louder.

Drums are probably the oldest and simplest musical instruments in the world. They contain a space filled with air, and have a flexible drumskin stretched across one end. When the drumskin is struck, it vibrates and makes a noise.

Although all drums work in basically the same way, they can still make a huge range of different noises. Size is important. A big bass drum makes a much deeper sound than a small bongo drum. The drum's pitch is also affected by the drumskin. A tight drumskin makes a higher note than a slack one.

MAKE it WORK!
Experiment with the sounds and tones of different drums. Try out some of these ideas and, if you like, put together a collection of drums to make your own drum kit.

You will need

string	thick paper
balloons	rubber bands
glue or sticky tape	thin wooden dowels

boxes and tins of all shapes and sizes
a sheet of plastic or an old plastic bag
an eyelet punch or cardboard hole reinforcers

▶ Bongo drums

1 Cut cardboard tubes into several different lengths, to make bongo drums that will sound different notes.

2 Cut some flat pieces of balloon rubber to make the drumskins, and fix across the tops of the cardboard tubes with elastic bands.

3 Attach a dowel to each drum. That way you can hang them up, and the notes will sound more clearly from the open ends of the drums.

▲ Tin-can drums
1 Take the lids off both ends of a tin can. Wash the tin, being very careful not to cut yourself on any sharp edges inside.

2 Stretch balloon rubber over the ends of the can, and secure it with elastic bands.

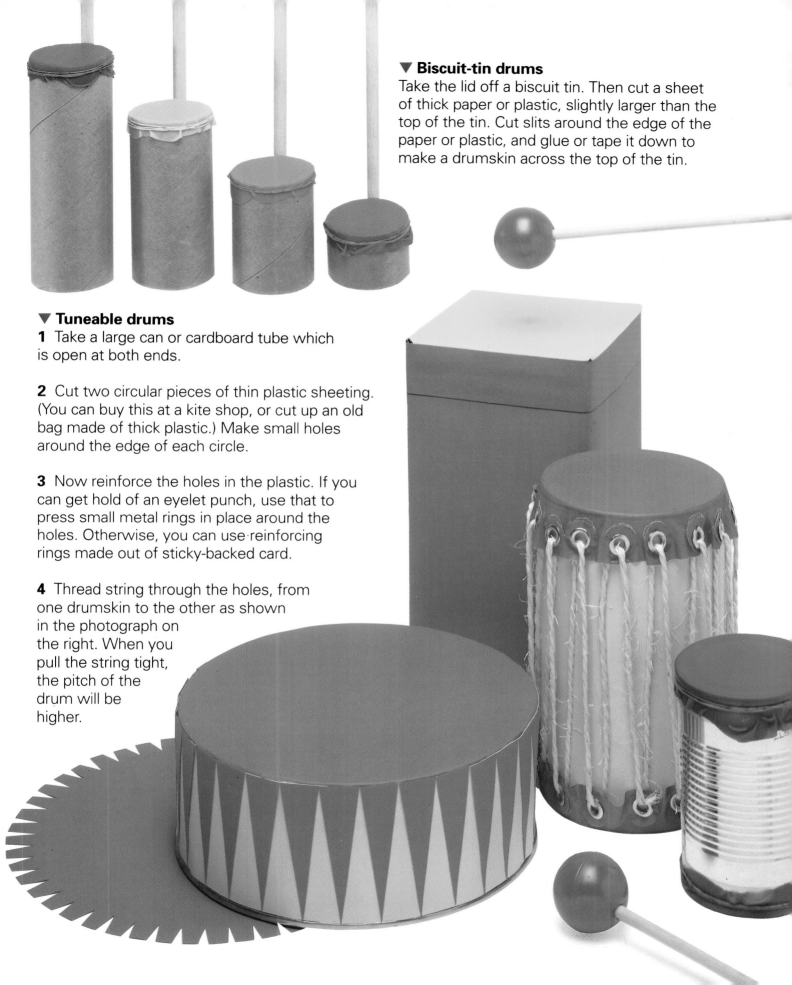

▼ Biscuit-tin drums

Take the lid off a biscuit tin. Then cut a sheet of thick paper or plastic, slightly larger than the top of the tin. Cut slits around the edge of the paper or plastic, and glue or tape it down to make a drumskin across the top of the tin.

▼ Tuneable drums

1 Take a large can or cardboard tube which is open at both ends.

2 Cut two circular pieces of thin plastic sheeting. (You can buy this at a kite shop, or cut up an old bag made of thick plastic.) Make small holes around the edge of each circle.

3 Now reinforce the holes in the plastic. If you can get hold of an eyelet punch, use that to press small metal rings in place around the holes. Otherwise, you can use reinforcing rings made out of sticky-backed card.

4 Thread string through the holes, from one drumskin to the other as shown in the photograph on the right. When you pull the string tight, the pitch of the drum will be higher.

Whirling rattles like the one on this page used to be a common sight at football matches. Groups of football supporters would wave their rattles to cheer on their team.

Our rattle makes a very loud noise. It creates sound in two different ways. The wooden surfaces of the cog and tongue make a clattering noise as they hit one another, while the whirling movement of the rattle sets off its own rhythmic pattern of sound vibrations in the air around it.

You will need

four metal washers   a cotton reel
a drill and hacksaw   strong wood glue
thin wooden dowelling
thick wooden dowelling
a fairly thick piece of wood (about 5 mm or ¼ in thick) for the frame of the rattle
thinner wood for the tongue of the rattle
matchsticks or thin slivers of wood

Be careful! This project involves some quite difficult woodworking. Ask an adult to help you with all the stages when you have to cut the wood or drill holes.

MAKE it WORK!

Make your own whirling rattle, take it out of doors and see how loud a noise you can make with it!

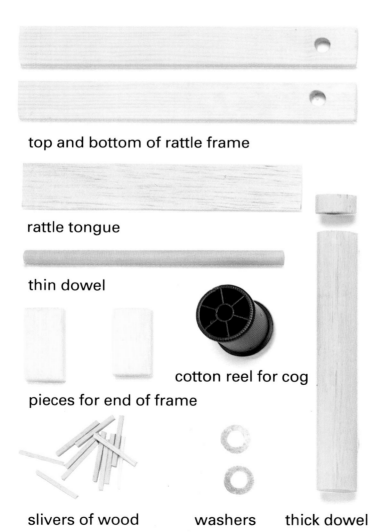

top and bottom of rattle frame

rattle tongue

thin dowel

cotton reel for cog

pieces for end of frame

slivers of wood   washers   thick dowel

1 Cut two identical oblong pieces out of the thicker wood. These will form the top and bottom of the frame of the rattle.

2 Cut an oblong of thin wood, slightly shorter than the width of the frame. This will be the tongue of the rattle.

3 Cut the thick dowel in two – you need a long piece for the handle of the rattle, and a much shorter piece for the top.

7 Assemble the rattle as shown in the photograph on the left. Thread the thin dowel through the cog and slip a washer on either side. Then add the top and bottom of the frame, followed by two more washers. Fit the ends of the thin dowel into the holes you have drilled in the thicker dowel.

8 Now glue the tongue and the outer end of the rattle in place. You must position the tongue very carefully. It should just touch the cotton-reel cog, so that it makes a noise, but should still be springy enough to let the cog spin around freely.

4 Cut two small rectangles of thick wood. They fit across the outer end of the rattle, with the tongue sandwiched between them.

5 Make the cog wheel. Cut several thin slivers of wood, or cut the heads off several matchsticks. Then glue these sticks around the side of the cotton reel, using strong wood glue.

6 Take a drill the same width as the thin wooden dowel. Drill a hole through one end of the top and bottom pieces of the frame. Then drill the same size holes into the centre of both pieces of thick wooden dowel.

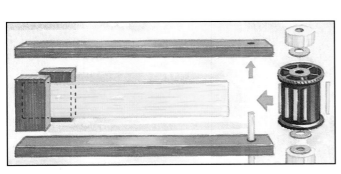

Assembling the whirling rattle

Be careful! Make sure that you use very strong wood glue to stick the pieces of the rattle together. Follow the instructions on the packet carefully, and try not to let the glue touch your skin.

The washers in the whirling rattle stop friction between the pieces of wood and help the rattle swing more easily.

Have you ever burst a balloon by accident? The loud, unexpected bang can make you almost jump out of your skin! The air trapped inside the balloon suddenly rushes out, setting off sound waves which we hear as a loud bang. The sound of any explosion is caused by air moving at great speed – that's why the sound blast from a bomb will knock over people and even buildings.

MAKE it WORK!

Moving air will make all sorts of noises. It can hum, whistle and whirr, as well as bang. Put together these simple cardboard gadgets and see how they crash like a thunder clap or hum like a bumble bee.

You will need

coloured card	glue
brown wrapping paper	string
scissors or a craft knife	a metal washer

Making a banger

1 Cut a square of card.

2 Cut another square of brown paper, slightly larger. Snip this square in half from corner to corner to make a triangle.

3 Place the brown paper on top of the card as shown, and fold it where it overlaps the card. Glue paper and card along the overlaps.

4 Fold both card and paper from corner to corner.

5 To make a sound, hold the corner of the banger as shown on the left. Sharply tug it downwards. The paper beak will flick out and make a bang.

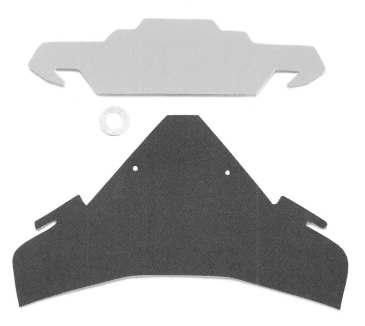

▲ Making a whirrer

1 Cut out the two cardboard shapes shown on the left, to make the wing and flapper sections. Slot them together.

2 Pierce two holes in the wing as shown, and glue a small metal washer to the nose to weight it down. Thread about a metre of string through the two holes.

3 Take the whirrer out of doors and spin it round your head. At first, the wing will just make a clattering noise, but as you speed up the sound will change to a high-pitched whirr.

▼ Making a spinner

1 Cut two hexagons of coloured card. Make two small holes at the centre, and four or five larger holes around the edges.

2 Glue the hexagons together. Thread a piece of string through the centre holes and tie the ends together.

3 Twist the string round and round. Then pull it outwards. As you pull, the string will keep on winding and unwinding itself and the spinner will keep on humming.

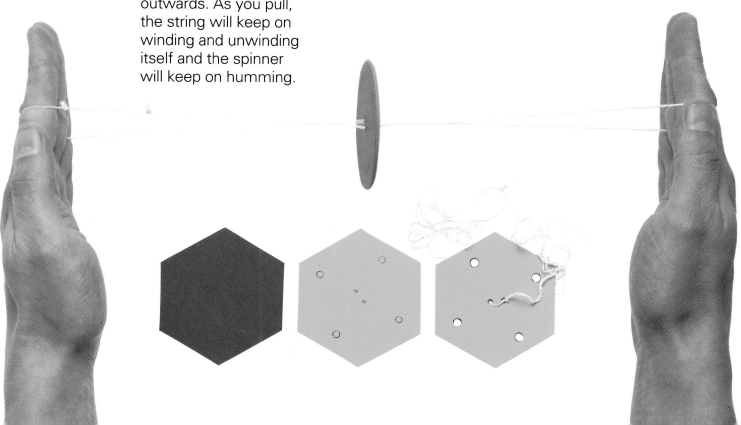

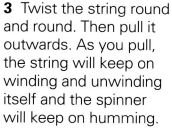

String instruments make music when a string or cord is plucked, so that the air around the string starts to vibrate. The pattern of a string instrument's sound waves depends on three things: the length of the string, what a string is made of and how tight it is.

A vibrating string on its own does not make much noise, and to make the sound louder, most string instruments have a **soundboard** and **resonator**. The soundboard picks up the strings' vibrations and transfers them to the resonator – a big space filled with air, which amplifies the sound.

You will need
an old tea chest
a broom handle
a hammer
string
a drill
nails

Make a tea-chest bass
Make your own instrument with one adjustable string and a tea-chest resonator.

1 Ask an adult to help you drill a hole in one corner of the tea chest. The broom handle should fit loosely inside the hole.

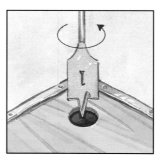

Drilling the hole

Fitting the handle

2 Tap nails into the opposite corner of the tea chest and the top of the broom handle. Tie a piece of string between the two nails.

3 Put one foot on the chest to hold it steady and pluck the string. Pull the handle back to tighten the string and make higher notes. Push it forwards for lower notes.

Make a stretched-string zither

Each string on this zither is stretched by the weight of a water bottle so that it makes its own individual note.

You will need

a hacksaw
a metal strip
food colouring
eight bottles of the same size
eight equal lengths of string or fine twine

a long wooden board
a hammer and nails

1 Tap a row of eight nails into the middle of the wooden board. Space them out equally across the board.

2 Ask an adult to help you cut a strip of metal the same width as the board. Make eight equally-spaced grooves in the strip.

3 Cut a groove across the wooden board, near one end, and wedge in the metal strip.

4 Dye the pieces of string in eight different colours with food dye. Fasten each string to a nail and run it across the metal strip and over the end of the board.

5 Tie the loose end of each string tightly around the neck of a bottle. Then pour a different amount of water into each bottle. The more water in a bottle, the tighter the string will be, and the higher its note. Try to make an octave scale.

6 Add food colouring to the water, to match the different strings.

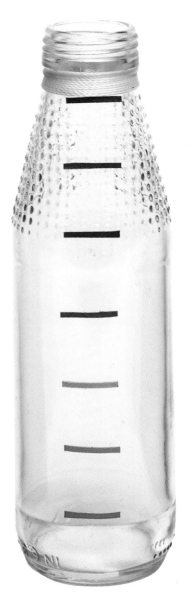

Playing strings

Many string instruments call for nimble fingers. Violinists or guitar players, for instance, hold down the strings in different places along the necks of their instruments. By altering the length of the strings they make different notes.

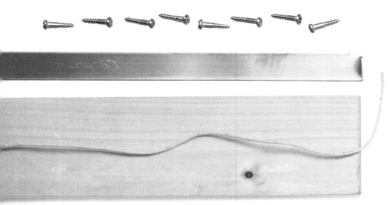

Make a banjo

This home-made banjo is almost like the real thing. It has a **bridge** to transfer the strings' vibrations to the soundboard, and a margarine tub which acts as a resonator. See how many different notes it will play.

You will need

a plastic tub
a strip of metal
wood and string
a bradawl and hacksaw
a screwdriver and screws

1 Cut a length of wood for the soundboard, about three times the width of the plastic tub.

2 Ask an adult to cut four small grooves in the metal strip, to make a bridge. Then cut another groove across the soundboard, near the bottom, and fix the bridge in it.

3 Mark holes in the wood where the screws will fit, following the photograph below. Twist the screws down a little way, and tie on the strings, leading them across the metal bridge.

4 Ask an adult to cut another piece of wood, the same depth as the plastic tub, to support the soundboard. Glue this support and the soundboard in place.

5 Twist the screws down further in order to tighten up the strings and fine tune the banjo.

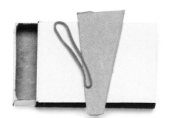 

Matchbox guitar

Stretch four rubber bands round a matchbox as shown on the left, and insert a bridge of thick card. The angle on the bridge means that each band is stretched by a different amount, so that it sounds a different note.

Making guitars

Rubber-band instruments are easy to make. Try either a large shoebox guitar, or the smaller, portable matchbox version.

Shoebox guitar

To make the shoebox guitar, just cut a hole in the lid, and stretch the bands across. Make the bridge from a sandwich of thick card and coloured paper as shown below. It should be so strong that you can slide it along to make the strings tighter.

You will need
a shoebox
matchboxes
a craft knife or scissors
rubber bands of all sizes
thick card and coloured paper

The shoebox guitar makes a deeper, richer sound than the little matchbox models, because the resonator is bigger and the strings (the rubber bands) are longer.

Nowadays, we can record music on cassettes or compact discs, but for hundreds of years, the only way of recording music was to write it down on paper. Over the centuries, a complicated system for writing music developed. This system of **musical notation** is now used for western music in many different countries.

The symbols and instructions on a **score** give all kinds of information to the musician – which notes to play and what rhythm to follow, how loud or soft, and how fast or slow the piece is. Learning to read and write music is like learning a new language.

▼ Western music is usually written on a set of five lines and four spaces called a **stave**. The positions of the notes on the stave tell the musicians which notes to play.

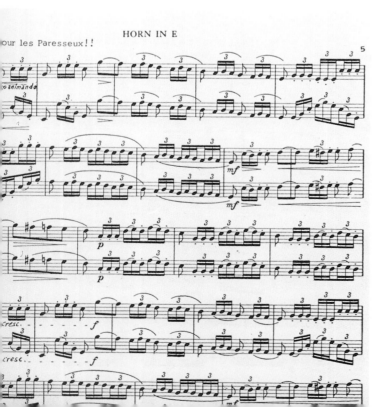

Some of the instructions on a musical score – especially those about the speed of a piece – are usually written in Italian. Andante, for instance, means slowly. Prestissimo means as fast as you can.

▲ To check that they are playing a piece at the right speed, musicians use a clockwork timer called a metronome. It has an upright pendulum that ticks backwards and forwards with a regular beat. By moving the weight up or down the pendulum, it can be made to tick more slowly or quickly.

MAKE it WORK!

You can work out your own simple system of writing down music and use it to record any music you compose for your home-made instruments.

1 Colour in the stick-on spots to match the colours of the stretched-string zither on page 41 or the bottle organ on page 26. The different coloured spots will stand for the different notes.

2 The size of the spots tells you how loudly to play the instrument. Small spots mean you play the note softly *(piano)*, medium-sized spots mean medium loud *(mezzo forte)* and large spots are loud *(forte)*.

You will need
graph paper
white stick-on spots in three sizes

▶ Here's a simple example, going up the octave scale and down again, not too loud and not too soft.

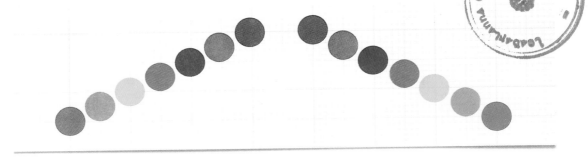

▶ Up and down the scale again. Softly on the way up, loudly on the way down.

▶ Music for two players. The line stands for a drum beat every other note. The guitar plays orange and red notes, getting louder and louder.

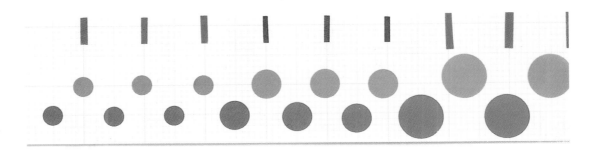

acid A word used by chemists to describe one of two kinds of chemical properties of certain substances. Acidic foods, such as lemons, taste sour or sharp. Strong acids are dangerous and can burn holes in wood or cloth.

aerial A long piece of wire or metal that picks up radio waves. All radios and televisions need an aerial.

alkaline A word used by chemists to describe one of two kinds of chemical properties of certain substances. In chemistry, an alkali is the opposite of an acid. One common kind of alkali is magnesia, the white liquid or powder we take to cure an upset stomach. Caustic soda is an example of a strong, dangerous alkali.

amplify When you amplify something, you make it louder.

atomic power Energy that comes from making changes to the centre of an atom. By splitting atoms, an enormous amount of heat is created. This heat is used to boil water, making steam to drive turbines and produce electricity.

atoms Tiny particles, over a million times smaller than the thickness of a human hair. Everything around us is made up of atoms — they are like building blocks, and by combining different atoms in different ways, different substances are created.

axle A rod or shaft around which wheels and gears turn.

ball bearings Ball bearings help to reduce friction when a wheel turns around an axle. The steel balls are placed so that they roll between the wheel and the axle.

bridge In a string instrument, the bridge is a small, raised piece of wood or metal that connects the strings to the soundboard.

cam An oval shape, or a wheel whose axle does not go through the centre. It is used to change a turning movement into an up-and-down movement.

circuit A loop-shaped path along which electricity can flow.

cochlea A curly tube inside the ear, filled with liquid and lined with tiny hairs. It turns the vibrations that sound waves make against the ear-drum into nerve pulses.

communications satellite A space-craft that goes around the Earth and that relays telephone conversations, fax messages and television pictures from one part of the world to another.

commutator A special kind of electrical connection, used in electric motors. A commutator makes the direction of the electric current change at regular intervals.

component In electronics, a component is one single part of a whole circuit. For example, a switch or a battery is a component in an electrical circuit.

compressed If something is compressed, it is squashed together by force. Compressed air stores energy that can be used to propel a model rocket.

conductor In electronics, a conductor is any substance that an electric current can pass through.

current electricity Current electricity is the electricity we use in homes, offices and factories. It is produced in power stations and is then distributed around the country through wires, pylons and transformers.

decibel A decibel is the unit for measuring how loud or soft a sound is.

diode A tube-shaped device used in electronic circuits. The diode stops the current flowing both ways through the circuit, making it flow in one direction.

drive belt A loop of rubber or material which carries power from one pulley to another.

drive chain A loop of chain which does the same job as a drive belt. The links of the chain fit around the teeth on gears called sprockets. A bicycle chain is an example of a drive chain.

eardrum The part of the ear inside the head that vibrates when struck by sound waves.

efficient An efficient machine does its job without wasting energy. Oil, for instance, helps many machines to run smoothly and efficiently by reducing the amount of friction that occurs between moving parts.

effort The force (a push or a pull) needed to work a lever or a pulley.

electrolyte A liquid solution that is able to conduct electricity. Batteries use electrolytes to make electricity.

electromagnets When an electric current passes through a metal, such as a piece of iron or copper, it always produces a magnetic field. Electro-magnets are especially useful because their magnetism can be switched on and off with the electric current.

electrons Tiny particles of atoms. Each electron carries an electrical charge.

electroscope A scientific instrument used to measure the strength of an electrical charge.

energy Energy is needed to do any kind of job or action. Motors and engines use energy, and so do our bodies. The energy stored in fuels such as petrol is used to power engines. People use the energy stored in their muscles for all physical activities. The food we eat and the electricity that powers an electric motor are both called energy sources.

engine A machine which uses the energy from a fuel, such as coal or petrol, to do work like lifting loads or turning wheels.

engineers Engineers use scientific knowledge to invent and make things. Besides machines, they design roads, bridges and buildings.

experiments An experiment is a trial to see whether something works. Scientists conduct experiments to test out their theories about how the world works.

filament A thin coil of wire, usually made from a substance called tungsten, inside a light bulb. The electricity has to work so hard to push its way through the tungsten that the coil glows and gives off light.

force A push or a pull, used to lift something, start it moving or hold it in place against another force such as gravity.

force field The area around a source of energy (such as a magnet) where the energy works.

fossil fuels Coal, oil and natural gas are fossil fuels. They are formed from the remains of ancient plants and animals, which have been buried for thousands of years beneath layers of mud and rock.

friction A dragging force which stops things sliding across each other smoothly. There is more friction on rough surfaces, such as sandpaper, than on smooth surfaces like ice. Friction produces heat (like when you rub yourself to keep warm)

and makes the two objects stick together (like tyres gripping the road).

fulcrum The hinge or pivot around which a lever turns.

gears Toothed wheels which link together and carry turning movement from one place to another. Gears are also used to change the speed and direction of movement.

generator A machine that turns heat or movement into an electrical current.

graphite The substance that pencil leads are made out of. Pencils contained lead until it was discovered that graphite was a better writing material.

gravity The force which makes objects fall towards the Earth and makes them feel heavy.

gyrocompass An instrument which always points in the same direction because it contains a spinning gyroscope.

hertz Sound waves are measured in a unit called the Hertz. It is named after the German physicist, Heinrich Hertz.

hub The centre of a wheel. The axle usually goes through the hub.

hydroelectric turbine A machine turned by flowing water, which is connected to an electricity generator.

hydroelectricity Electricity produced by the energy of water flowing through a generator.

incus One of the three main bones inside the ear. Often also called the anvil bone.

insulators Materials that do not conduct electricity. Rubber and plastic are both good insulators.

lever A rod or bar which rests on a pivot. A load at one end of the lever can be lifted by applying an effort at the other end.

load The weight or force which is moved by applying an effort to a lever or pulley. The part of an electric circuit that uses the electric power is also called a load. In a lighting circuit, the load is the light bulb.

malleus One of the bones inside the ear. It is often also called the hammer bone.

matter All the different substances in the Universe are 'matter'. There are three forms: solids, liquids or gases.

molecule A tiny particle of a substance. Every molecule is made up of two or more atoms joined together.

mesh The teeth on two gears are meshed when they fit together. One gear turns and its teeth mesh with the teeth on the second gear and make it turn too.

musical notation Recording music by writing it down on paper.

nerve pulses Nerve pulses are signals sent out by our organs of sense, such as our eyes and ears. These signals pass along our nerves, to the brain, where they are decoded as sights, sounds, tastes, smells or feelings.

note In music, a note is a sound played at a particular pitch.

octave An octave is a scale of eight notes that rise and fall step by step. Most western music is based on this octave scale.

pendulum A hanging weight, which swings to and fro because of the force of gravity.

percussion instruments Musical instruments that are played by being struck or shaken. Drums, maracas and xylophones are all examples of percussion instruments.

phonograph An early kind of record player. It recorded sounds by making a series of bumps and dips in grooves on a rotating cylinder.

physics The branch of science that finds out about different kinds of energy and matter. Sound is one of the forms of energy investigated by physicists.

pitch The pitch of a note is how high or how low it is. If sound waves are close together they make a higher pitch than if they are far apart.

pivot A hinge or balance point, around which something turns.

pneumatic Pneumatic machines are driven by compressed air.

pollution Waste or rubbish which damages the natural world around us.

projectile A missile thrown by a catapult or fired from a cannon.

pulley A wheel turned by a rope or drive belt. It changes the direction of a force, or carries it from one place to another.

pulley blocks Two or more pulleys joined together to lift a large load with a small effort.

radio waves Waves of electro-magnetic energy that travel rapidly across long distances. Sounds are turned into radio waves by a radio transmitter, and changed back into sound again by a radio receiver.

range The distance travelled by a projectile between being fired and landing.

resistor A substance which offers resistance to an electric current. The current has to work hard to get through a resistor, so resistors are put into circuits to reduce the voltage of the current.

resonator A space inside an instrument filled with air, which vibrates and makes the sound of the instrument louder.

rotate To turn around, like a wheel on an axle.

scale A series or sequence of different musical notes.

scientist Someone who studies the world in a systematic way, to try and understand how it works.

score A written record of a piece of music.

silicon chip A tiny, wafer-thin slice of the substance silicon, which has a whole electronic circuit on it, in miniature. Silicon chips are an especially important part of modern computers.

sound waves Sounds travel through the air in waves. When someone bangs on a drum, for example, the drumskin squashes together the air beside it every time it vibrates. If we could see air, the movement of sound waves would look rather like the ripples on a pond when a stone is thrown into the water.

soundboard The board in a piano or a string instrument which is connected to the strings by the bridge. It vibrates when the strings are struck or plucked.

sprockets Toothed wheels, connected by a drive chain (see separate entry).

stapes One of the bones of the inner ear. It is often also called the stirrup bone.

static electricity Static electricity is an electrical charge which is produced naturally when two things rub together. Lightning is the best-known example of static electricity.

stave In music, a stave is a set of five lines on which musical notes are written.

stethoscope An instrument used by a doctor to listen to the inside of a patient's body.

string instruments String instruments are played by plucking strings or scraping them with a bow.A sitar, a zither, a violin and a guitar are all examples of string instruments.

terminals The points in an electrical circuit where the electric current leaves or enters the circuit.

theory An idea which tries to explain something. Scientific theories usually have to be proved by experiments before they are said to be true.

trajectory The curved path that a projectile follows as it travels through the air.

vacuum A completely empty space that does not even contain air. Outer space is a vacuum.

vibrate When something vibrates, it moves backwards and forwards a small amount very quickly. A guitar string vibrates if you pluck it.

wind instruments Instruments that are played by blowing through them. Trumpets and recorders are both wind instruments.

Air-beds 32
amplifiers 104, 130
Ancient Egyptians 59
Ancient Greeks 72, 76, 77
Archimedean screws 28
Archimedes 28
argon 63
atomic power 50
atoms 52, 72
axles 24, 31, 37

Balance 99
ball bearings 16, 17
banjos 132
bats, hearing range of 94, 97, 110, 111, 112
batteries 51, 56–57
battery tester 57
Bell, Alexander Graham 104
bicycle chains 21
bicycles 18, 20, 33
bob sleighs 17
boosting power 90–91
bottle openers 9
brain 98, 100, 106
bridges 132, 133

Cam shaft 24, 25
cams 24–25, 29
can openers 6
candle clocks 46

car engines 34, 43
catapults 10–11, 33, 38
centrifugal force 91
circuits 54–55, 58, 60–65, 66, 70–71
clocks 6, 20, 44–47
candle clocks 46
marble clocks 44–45
pendulum clocks 47
sand clocks 46
water clocks 47
cochlea 98, 99
coin battery 57
combine harvesters 29
commutator 84, 85
compasses 78, 79
computers 70
conductors 54, 55

Decibels 104, 105
diodes 114, 115
dogs, hearing range of 97
drive belts 18–19, 20
drive chains 21
drums 94, 95, 96, 106, 118, 124–125
Dunlop, John 33

Ear 95, 96, 98–99, 100, 101, 102, 104, 105, 106, 107
cochlea 98, 99
eardrum 97, 98, 99
incus 98, 99

malleus 98, 99
stapes 98, 99
ear trumpets 104, 105
eardrum 97, 98, 99
echoes 110
Edison, Thomas 63, 109
effort 8, 9, 16
electric motor 51, 84–90
electric trains 88–89
electricity 37
electrodes 56
electromagnetism 82–83, 84–85
electrons 52, 53, 54, 55, 64, 74
electroscope 52
energy 34, 36, 38, 39
engineers 6
engines 6, 34
car engines 34, 43
rubber-band engines 38–41
steam engines 42–43
explosions 128

Fans 19
filament 62, 63
fluorescent bulbs 63
force 7, 15, 16, 36
force field 74, 76, 78, 80
friction 16, 17, 18
fuel 34
fulcrums 8, 9

Galilei, Galileo 47
gears 20–23, 24
generators 58
graphite 67
gravity 26, 27, 28, 30,
    31, 40
gravity screws 26–27,
    34
guitars 132, 133, 135
gunpowder 10
gyrocompasses 31
gyroscopes 31

Hearing 97, 99,
    100–101, 104, 110
Hertz 97
horse power 43
hovercraft 87
hubs 16
hydroelectric turbine 37
hydroelectricity 37, 50,
    58

Ice skates 16
incus 98, 99
insulators 54
iron filings 80

Levers 8–9, 10, 12–13,
    15
light bulbs 51, 62–63
light waves 97, 101
lighthouses 58–59

lightning 53, 101
lines of force 80
load 8, 9, 15, 55

Magnetic fields
    see force fields
magnets, magnetism
    51, 72–81, 84–85
malleus 98, 99
maracas 122
marble clocks 44–45
mechanical diggers 12
megaphones 105
metal recorders 96, 110
metronomes 134
microphones 95, 108,
    109
molecules 72
Morse code 67, 68–69
Morse, Samuel 68
music 94, 103,
    116–118, 134–135

Negative charge 52–53,
    56
neon bulbs 63
nitrogen 63
nuclear fuel 58

Octave 116, 117, 118,
    131, 135
oil 17, 36
outer space 97

Panpipes 118, 120
pantograph 12, 13
parallel circuit 60
pencil sharpeners 7
pendulum clocks 47
pendulums 30, 47
percussion instruments
    119, 122–123
petrol 25, 36, 41
Pharos of Alexandria 59
physics 50
pipes 118–119, 120,
    121
pitch 96, 116, 117, 118,
    124, 125
    high 96, 97, 110, 121
    low 96
pivots 8, 10, 11
pneumatic tyres 32, 33
poles (of magnets) 78,
    80, 84
Poles (of the Earth) 78
pollution 36
popcorn dispenser 28,
    29
positive charge 52–53,
    56
power stations 58, 90
projectile 10, 11
pulley blocks 15
pulleys 14–15, 18

Radio waves 114–115
radios 70
rattles 122, 123,
    126–127
recorders 120, 121

recording sound
108–109
reflecting sound
102–103, 108
resistance, resistors 67
resonators 130, 132,
133
rockets 6, 34–35
roller blinds 14
rotation 18–19, 20, 21,
22, 23
rubber-band engines
38–41
rubber boots 16

Sand clocks 46
scales 116, 117, 118,
131, 135
scores 134
screws 29
Archimedean screws
28
gravity screws 26–27,
34
see-saws 8
series circuits 60
silence 105
silicon chips 70
slide whistle 120,
121
sound horns 108
sound waves 94–97, 99,
102–106, 108,
110–112, 114, 116,
119, 128,
130
soundboards 130, 132

sprockets 21
stapes 98, 99
starter motors 19
static electricity 52–53,
54, 72
stave 134
steam engines 42–43
stethoscopes 104
string instruments
130–134
switches 66–67

Tape recorders 95, 108
telephones 95,
106–107, 114
terminals 54
thunder 101, 105
trajectory of flight 11,
33
trombones 120
tubular bells 119
tuning forks 117
turbines 37

Vacuum 97
Volta, Count Alessandro
57
volts 59

Water clocks 47
water pumps 29
water wheels 36, 37
watts 59, 62–63

weighing scales 9
whales, hearing of 95,
102
wheelbarrows 8
wheels 16, 22, 24, 27
wind instruments 118,
119, 120–121
windmills 36, 37

Zithers 131, 135